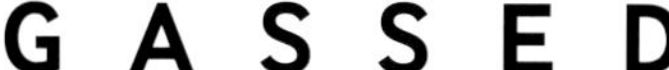
GASSED

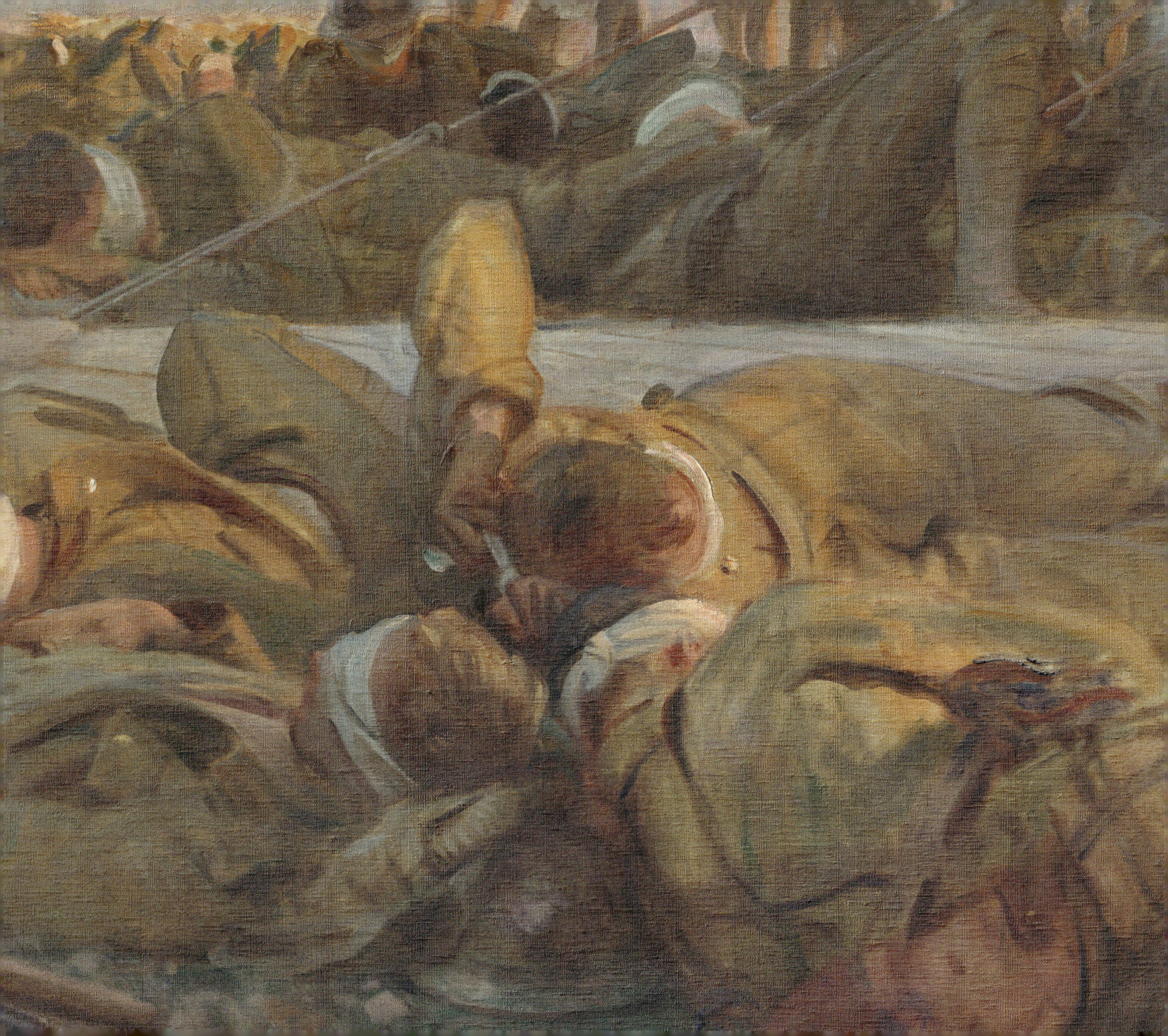

JOHN SINGER SARGENT'S

GASSED

REBECCA NEWELL

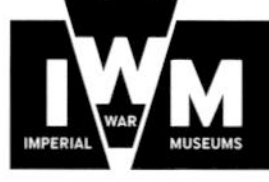

John Singer Sargent's *Gassed* is one of IWM's most iconic and best-loved objects. Truly monumental in scale, it is also the largest painting in the museum's collection and has been on near-constant display since it was first exhibited in 1919. A favourite among visitors and the most requested image by researchers and publishers, the work endures as a lasting symbol of modern art in public service, and of the transformative conflict from which it came.

In the following pages IWM's Head of Art Rebecca Newell traces the origins of this large and powerful painting in the final months of the First World War and celebrates the vibrancy and visual power of the work, revealed once again during recent conservation. *John Singer Sargent's Gassed* reflects on the challenges of creating and displaying a canvas of such size and the dramatic impact the work has had on generations of visitors to IWM. Finally, the book considers the painting's enduring legacy in the context of art inspired by conflict – a legacy now secured for future generations.

Published by IWM, Lambeth Road, London SE1 6HZ
iwm.org.uk

ISBN 978-1-912423-71-2

A catalogue record for this book is available from the British Library.
Printed and bound by Gomer Press Limited
Colour reproduction by DL Imaging

Front and back cover: John Singer Sargent, *Gassed*, 1919
Pages 6, 8, 16, 36, 37, 38 and 70: Details of John Singer Sargent, *Gassed*, 1919

CONTENTS

PREFACE 7

FOREWORD 9

'A GREAT AND LASTING SERVICE' 17

TIMELINE 36

THE CREATION AND DISPLAY OF *GASSED* 39

PRESERVING FOR THE FUTURE 71

NOTES 98

PICTURE CREDITS 99

ABOUT THE AUTHOR 100

ACKNOWLEDGEMENTS 100

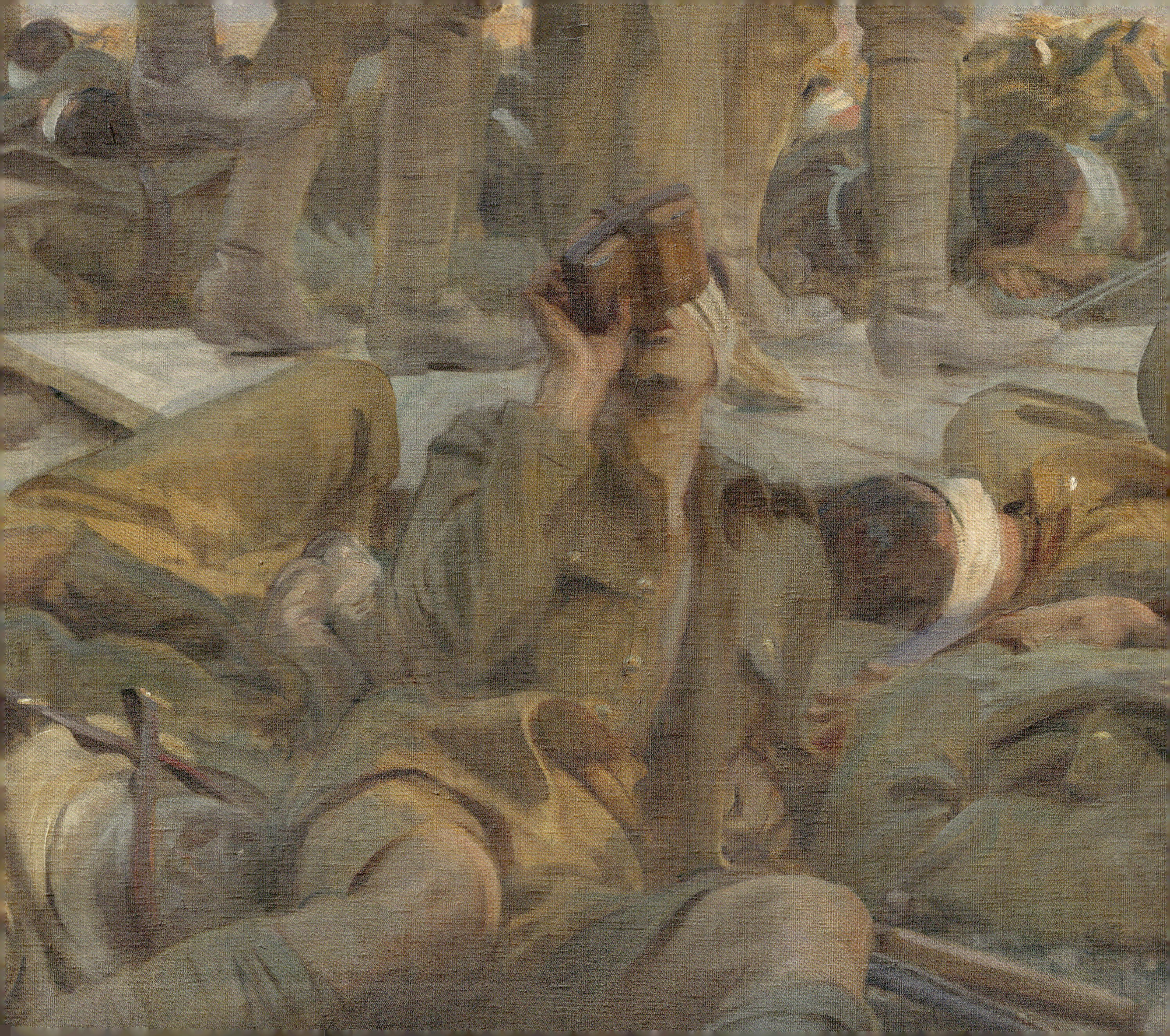

PREFACE

Caro Howell
Director-General, IWM

Central to the new Blavatnik Art, Film and Photography Galleries is *Gassed*, the monumental painting by John Singer Sargent. One of the most iconic and best-loved objects in IWM's collection, *Gassed* has been on near-constant display since it was first exhibited at the Royal Academy in 1919, two years after the Imperial War Museum was founded.

Over the years discoloured varnish has obscured Sargent's intention and skewed our reading of his work. However, as part of creating the new Galleries we took the opportunity to conserve and clean the painting – a significant undertaking given its immense scale. Discoveries made during this year-long process about the creation, meaning and place of *Gassed* within Sargent's wider practice are explored by Rebecca Newell, IWM's Head of Art, and writer and curator Richard Ormond in the following pages.

One element of the work that cleaning has brought strikingly to the fore is Sargent's articulation of the sensory world that the newly blinded troops are navigating. Freed from the mustard pall of old varnish, the painting's delicate palette of pinks, mauves and blues captures the stillness of the air and, by extension, the sounds it carries. We, like the young men with bandaged eyes, register the soft nasal rasp of the biplanes overhead, the shouts of instruction and encouragement of football players, the thud of boot on ball and, all around, the small, quiet sounds of exhaustion – water in a canteen, creaking leather, clinking rifles and helmets, low groans and the shuffle of bodies in wool. Against the air's cool hues, the patches of light from the dying sun catch our attention too, evoking their weak warmth on exposed skin and through uniforms. Finally, with Sargent's bravura brushwork now fully visible, the contrast with the wounded men's hesitant and misjudged steps is all the more poignant.

I would like to thank conservators Phil Young and Hans Thompson of Orbis Conservation for their dedication and expertise, and for the hugely privileged access they gave the IWM team while the painting was in the studio. We are also grateful to Richard Ormond for his continued interest in *Gassed* and its place in our collection; to Factum, whose state-of-the-art digital preservation technology has provided remarkable new insights into the canvas, which audiences around the world can now access online; and to our colleagues in the sector, including Tate, for their support and interest in our conservation work.

Finally I would like to thank the Blavatnik Family Foundation, whose generosity brought the new Galleries into being, and the Foyle Foundation for their generous support of the beautiful *Mind and Body* space. Here we may consider not only Sargent's masterpiece, but also the ongoing power of artists, filmmakers and photographers to shape how we think and feel about conflict.

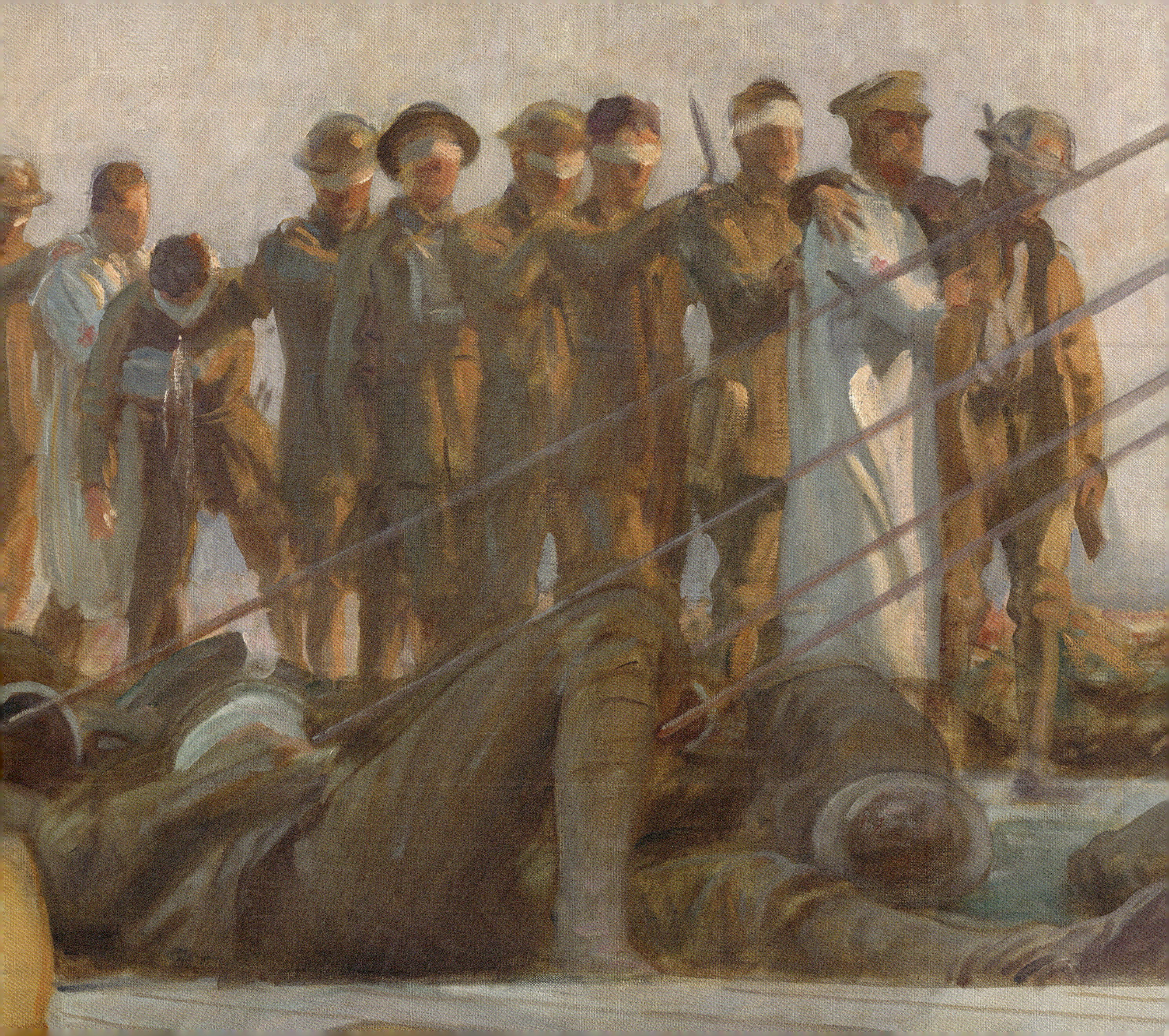

FOREWORD

Richard Ormond
Art Historian

Gassed is a great emblematic painting, a profound statement about the suffering and sacrifice of war. At the same time it is deeply human, alive to the individuality of the soldiers blinded by mustard gas who constitute its subject. The setting is a glorious evening sunset in which the golden light acts as a foil to the agony of the men and the horrors of war. An encampment of tents and a game of football are to be seen in the distant background; tiny aeroplanes buzz about the sky. Symbolism is here allied to the specifics of a given time and place, recorded with that deep feeling for the flow of life and the play of light that are such hallmarks of Sargent's art. He was a proto-Impressionist, a lifelong friend of Claude Monet and other progressive French artists, and he had the gift of investing the scenes he recorded with the force and reality of the moment.

Such was Sargent's fame that it took a letter from the prime minister David Lloyd George to persuade him to accept a commission for the work. On an earlier occasion he had turned down the opportunity of painting Edward VII's coronation, citing his lack of experience, and

→

John Singer Sargent, *A Street in Arras*, 1918

WATERCOLOUR ON PAPER

When Sargent arrived in France in July 1918, he spent time with the Guards Division near Arras and with the American Expeditionary Forces near Ypres. This scene depicts Scottish troops resting against the exterior wall of a shell-damaged building, their rifles against the wall beside them. The composition is divided between the view into the coach house and the scene in the street. The hole brutally blasted into the wall shows the remains of a carriage lying among the rubble from the roof. Sargent's study of the effects of weaponry is all the more powerful because of his attention to architectural detail.

he might well have said the same about a war picture. However, the conflict had deeply affected Sargent; he had lost his favourite niece and model Rose-Marie Ormond in 1918 and he had supported numerous wartime charities. He experienced the impact of the war personally when he became trapped in the Austrian Tyrol in August 1914 and had considerable difficulty extricating himself. Sargent further courted danger by crossing the Atlantic twice, in 1916 and 1918.

The British War Memorials Committee (BWMC), an offshoot of the Ministry of Information, had plans for a post-war Hall of Remembrance in which a 20-foot painting by Sargent was to be one of the centrepieces. The large-scale paintings for the Hall were intended to reflect the heroism and sacrifice of war rather than serving as documents of specific engagements. Influenced by Sargent's American citizenship, the Committee suggested to him that he might like to paint a subject of Anglo-American co-operation.

And so with this in mind Sargent departed for the front early in July 1918; he was accompanied by a close friend, the artist and art teacher Henry Tonks. There he was successively billeted with British and American command centres. The war fired his imagination and he set about recording in watercolour the scenes by which he was surrounded: mangled tanks and machinery, even a solitary crashed aeroplane; damaged buildings; trenches and encampments; resting and bathing 'Tommies', and another two of them stealing fruit; horses and mules; rows of army lorries both moving and stationary; and the interior of a hospital tent, which Sargent experienced himself when struck down by a bout of 'flu. In the course of three months the artist managed to complete over 35 watercolours as well as a magisterial oil painting of the shattered interior of Arras Cathedral.

Meanwhile the subject matter for his war artist commission hung fire. As he wrote to a friend, the nearer he got to the front the less there was to see. He did three oil sketches of the meeting of American and British troops, the former marching blithely to the front while their wounded and exhausted counterparts head in the opposite direction. Another idea he explored was that of flat-iron railway

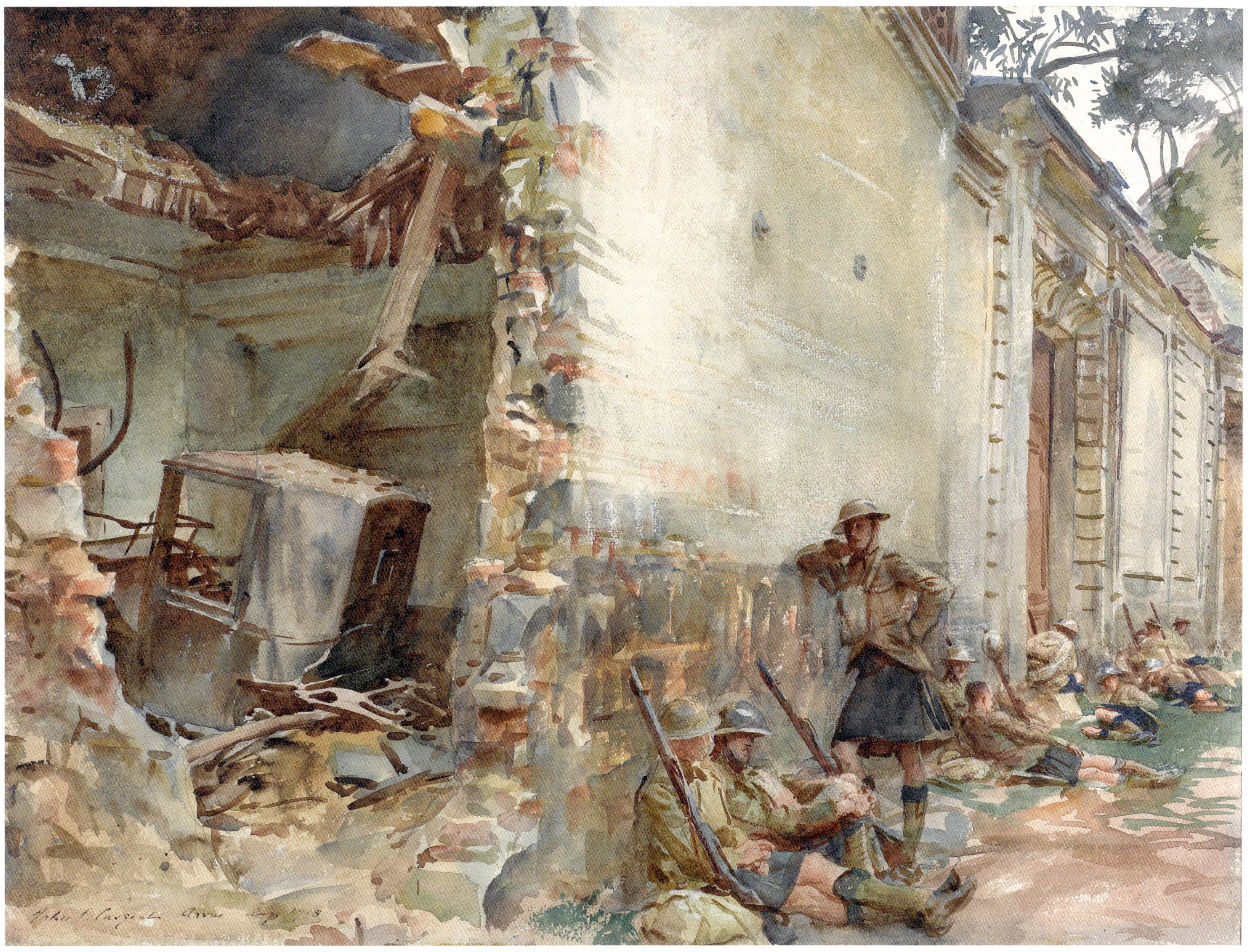

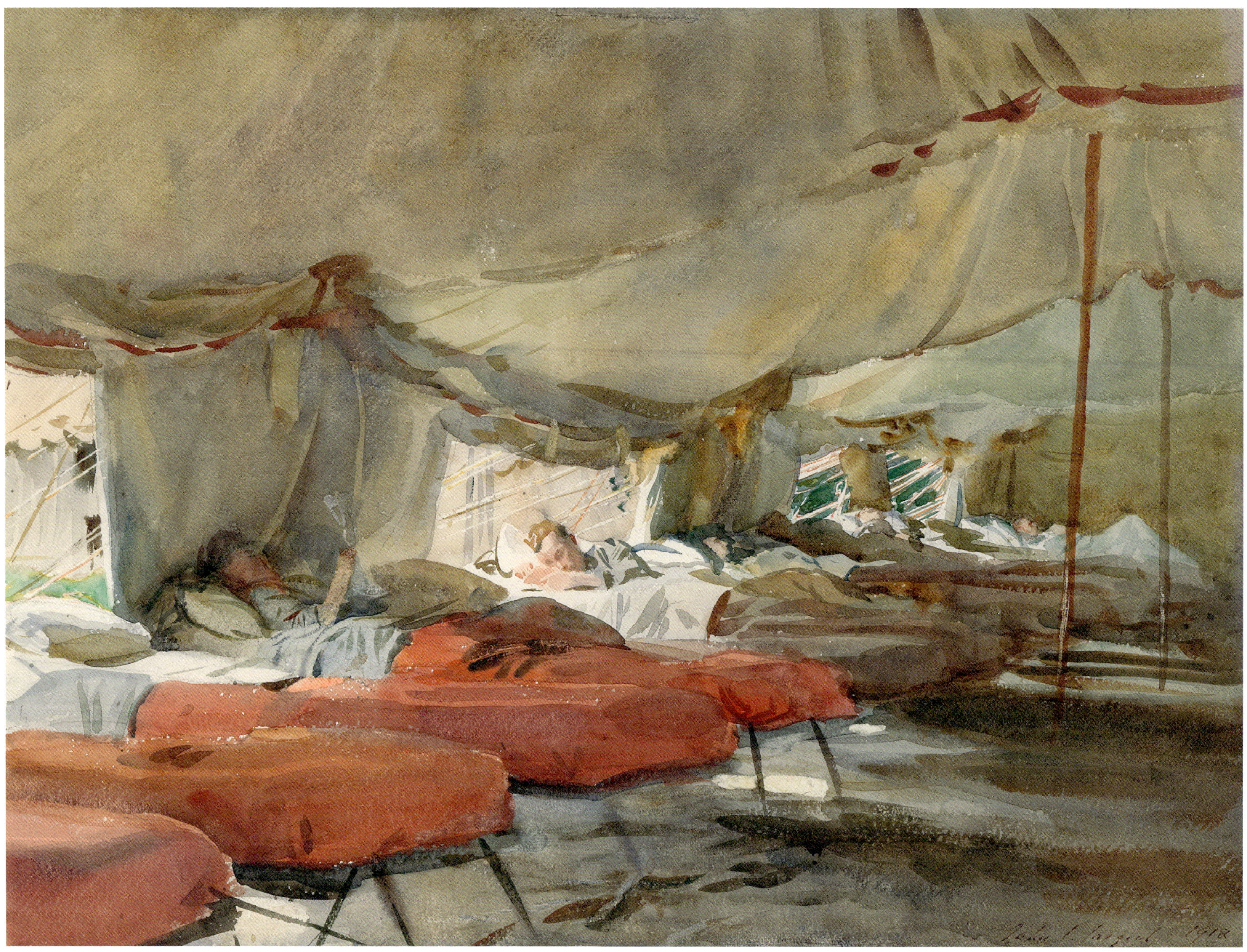

←

John Singer Sargent,
***The Interior of a Hospital Tent,* 1918**

WATERCOLOUR ON PAPER

Late in September 1918, while gathering material for *Gassed* near Péronne, Sargent was struck down with influenza and taken to a hospital near Roisel. Here he spent a week in a hospital bed next to wounded troops, which inspired this work. In a letter to Isabella Stewart Gardner, Sargent wrote of fitful nights spent there with 'the accompaniment of groans of wounded, and the choking and coughing of gassed men, which was a nightmare'. Many parts of a field hospital, from wards to operating theatres, were housed in tents during the First World War.

John Singer Sargent,
***Thou Shalt Not Steal,* 1918**

WATERCOLOUR ON PAPER

This evocative watercolour, in which Sargent depicts British soldiers picking apples in an orchard, offers a more explicitly Impressionist consideration of colour and light. It was painted during Sargent's billeting in Arras shortly after his arrival in France. The soldier on the left bites into the fruit while looking furtively around, while his companion reaches up to pick from the higher branches.

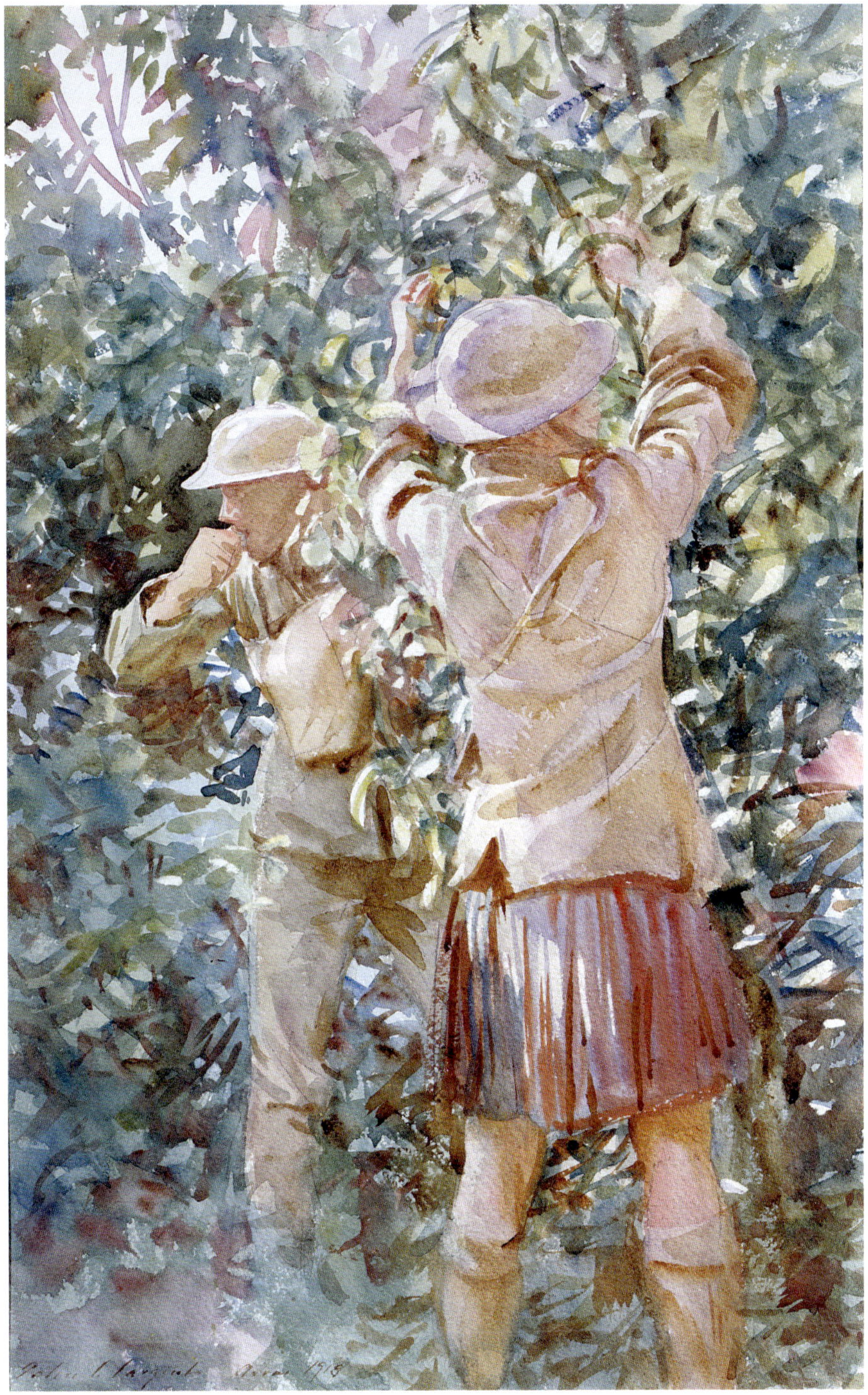

→
John Singer Sargent,
***Ruined Cathedral, Arras,* August 1918**
OIL ON CANVAS

Sargent was stationed in Arras when he arrived in France in 1918. While searching for the subject for his commission, he produced not only 35 watercolours of people and scenes around him, but also this commanding oil painting of the ruins of Arras Cathedral. Sargent's depiction is a shimmering Impressionist study of colour and light, with bright sun streaming in through the skeletal cathedral structure. Piles of debris – including classical pilaster capitals and a decapitated statue – rest below.

The Cathedral had been badly damaged during heavy German shelling in April 1917 in the run up to the Franco-British Nivelle offensive, which aimed to penetrate the German front line. Sargent's decision to commit the scene of the damaged building to oil paint suggests its significant impact on the artist.

trucks carrying a dense crowd of American troops up the line. Then, quite out of the blue, he saw the scene he was to immortalise – a group of British casualties, blinded by a German mustard gas attack, making their way in small groups to a dressing station at Bac-du-Sud on the Arras–Doullens road. Sargent had found the motif he needed and he faced down the BWMC, telling them that he would only do a 20-footer for a subject of his choosing.

He came back to London as the war ended to start work on his big picture. As an experienced muralist, the huge scale and complexity of the work on which he was engaged held no terrors for him. The slow-moving line of soldiers at the centre of Sargent's composition, arms rhythmically stretched to shoulders, has the character of a tragic requiem. On either side of this procession, classical in its composition, lie the suffering and entangled bodies of those who have already been treated. Guy ropes on the right indicate the unseen dressing station.

The picture was painted in one of the artist's Fulham Avenue studios, where he employed a succession of models to make detailed studies of the standing and sleeping figures. While such studies are part and parcel of the academic process, those by Sargent remain vibrant in style and character. More than 20 such studies are recorded and I can claim a personal connection with them. A dozen had been lent to the Imperial War Museum by my great-aunt Emily Sargent, sister of the artist. She had died in 1936 and there they had remained. In 1987 I persuaded my siblings and cousins to do the decent thing and donate the drawings to the institution in her memory.

Having worked out the composition and held it in his mind's eye, Sargent set to work with a will. The brushwork is unlaboured and uninhibited, swept in with broad strokes of paint. No doubt it was accompanied by those mutterings and imprecations recorded by his sitters ('Demons! Demons!') as he struggled to realise his vision. His experience with paint saw him through – that alliance of hand and eye that enabled him to paint *au premier point*, as the French would say, with the dash and confidence that made him such a master. And the recent, first-rate conservation of the picture by Phil Young underlines this painterliness. Layers of discoloured varnish have been peeled away to reveal a fresh and light-filled canvas, like a butterfly emerging from a chrysalis. A wonderfully clear light ripples through the foreground figures, emphasising their huddled, contorted, interlocking bodies. By contrast the processing soldiers are mostly in shadow, silhouetted against a shimmering sky – an Impressionist mosaic of tiny dashes of colour that had been lost prior to conservation. We can now enjoy the sensual and pictorial qualities of the canvas as Sargent intended, while responding to the tragic nature of its subject.

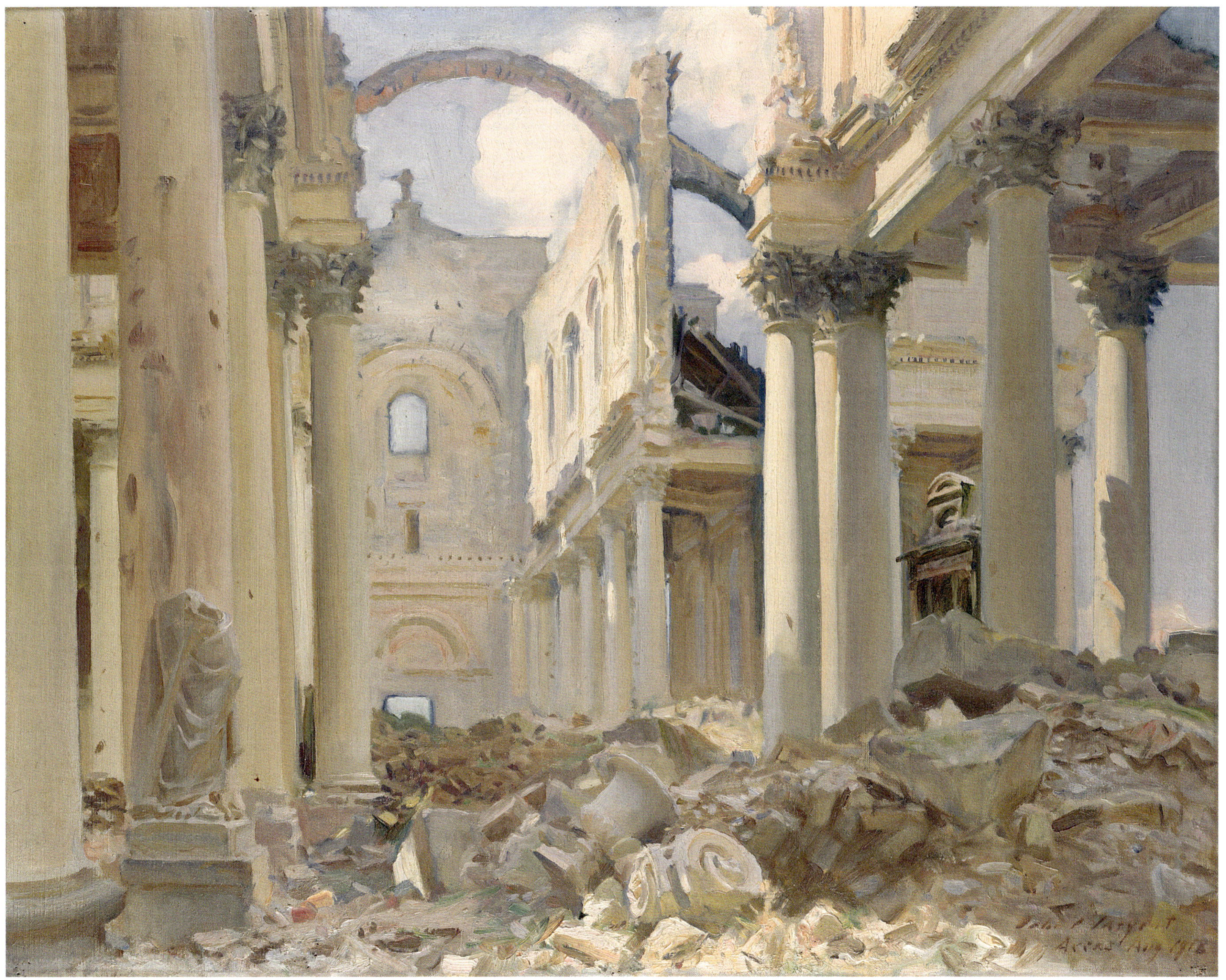

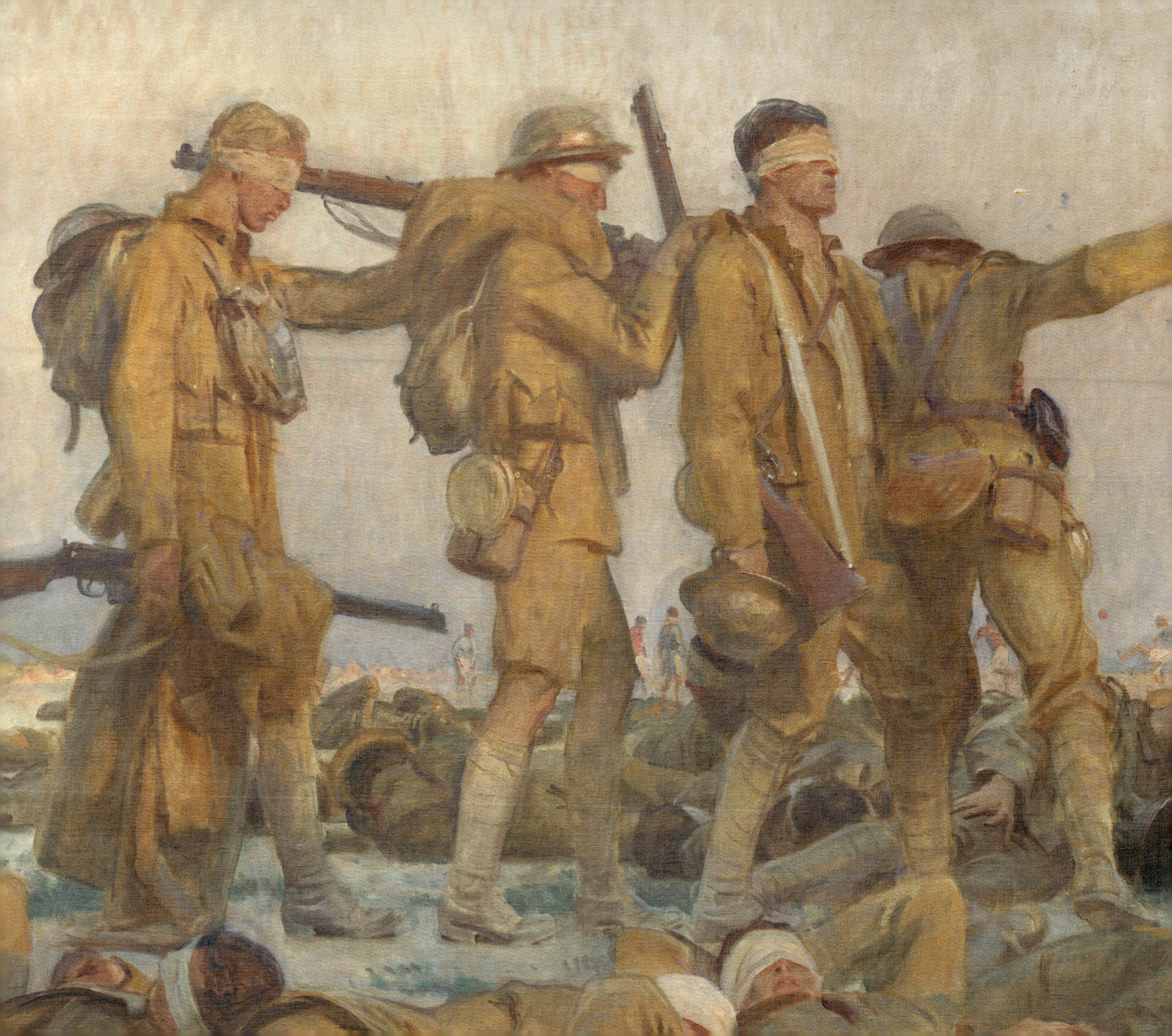

‘A GREAT AND LASTING SERVICE’

John Singer Sargent’s *Gassed* is an exceptional painting. Made in 1918, different to anything the artist had produced before, it was commissioned by the government as the centrepiece of a newly imagined national memorial to the unprecedented experience and loss of the First World War. It is truly monumental in scale – the largest painting in IWM’s collection, a favourite among visitors and the museum’s most requested image by researchers and publishers. The work endures as an iconic symbol of modern art in public service, and of the transformative conflict from which it came.

The scene for *Gassed* is the medical aftermath of a mustard gas attack on the Western Front. A line of soldiers with bandaged eyes are led along by an orderly; each man holds the shoulder of the soldier in front. One soldier turns away from the viewer to vomit. A football match plays on in the background, alluding to the routine nature of such attacks.

The first use of poison gas on the Western Front occurred at Ypres in April 1915, when the Germans released clouds of chlorine. This was followed by phosgene later the same year, and then by mustard gas in summer 1917. Soldiers feared gas. Chlorine and phosgene choked and suffocated them, while mustard gas caused burns, blisters and (usually temporary) blindness. Mustard gas was the most effective of the weapons, causing eight times as many British casualties than any other. However, in part due to the improvements in gas masks and medical treatment, poison gas caused few casualties compared to artillery. As the war progressed some 185,000 British soldiers became victims of gas, which killed about 3 per cent of those affected.[1]

Gassed depicts a scene rooted in the contemporary moment and the horror of this new weapon. Yet in Sargent’s frieze-like structure and masterful exercise in foreshortening, he also roots it consciously in a representational history of blindness. Pieter Bruegel the Elder’s *The Parable of the Blind,* painted in 1568, is a significant reference point.

Shortly after it was completed, Sargent’s *Gassed* was recognised as an era-defining painting and as a chronicle of ordinary – and extraordinary – conflict experience. It was included in the Summer

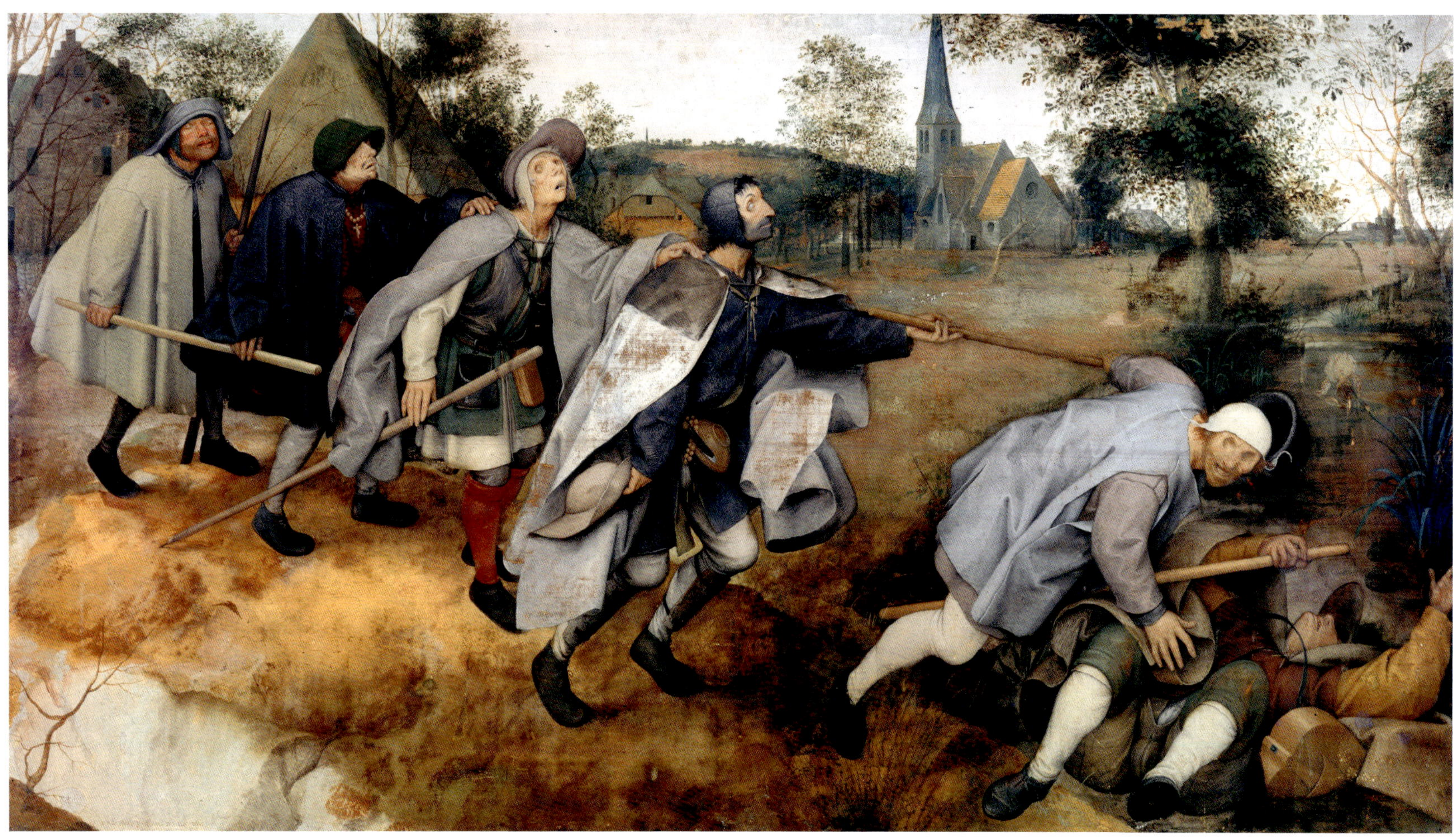

↑
Pieter Bruegel the Elder,
***The Parable of the Blind,* 1568**

TEMPERA ON LINEN CANVAS
MUSEO DI CAPODIMONTE, NAPLES

This unflinching depiction of blindness is based on a biblical parable. It is likely that John Singer Sargent had this painting in mind while working on the composition of *Gassed*.

In the painting Bruegel presents a line of six blind men linked by their staffs. Each man holds his head aloft, suggesting that their other senses are heightened; their mis-stepping is exaggerated. The diagonal composition reinforces the off-kilter motion of the figures as they fall in progression. Bruegel achieved masterful accuracy in the rendering of detail and foreshortening. The eye conditions are depicted with such realism that they are identifiable: corneal leukoma, eyeball atrophy and removed eyes.

Bruegel's formation of a frieze of figures across the middle ground of the canvas and muted palette bear comparison with *Gassed*. The fallen figure on the far right recalls the soldier drinking from his water bottle in the foreground of Sargent's painting. In *Gassed*, walking staffs are replaced with rifles.

↑
John Singer Sargent, *Study for Gassed: line of wounded men with medical orderly, c.*1918

PENCIL ON PAPER

This is a preparatory study of the second line of gassed British soldiers depicted in *Gassed*. The group is made up of eight soldiers led by a medical orderly; one of the rearmost soldiers leans over to vomit. In the top left is a study of a medical orderly holding the right arm of a gassed soldier.

Sargent was interested in producing an epic with 'masses of men' following the suggestion, from the British War Memorials Committee (BWMC), to produce a work on the subject of the co-operation between British and American forces. Following the precedent of Bruegel, Sargent draws the viewer from left to right into the tactile relationships between the men.

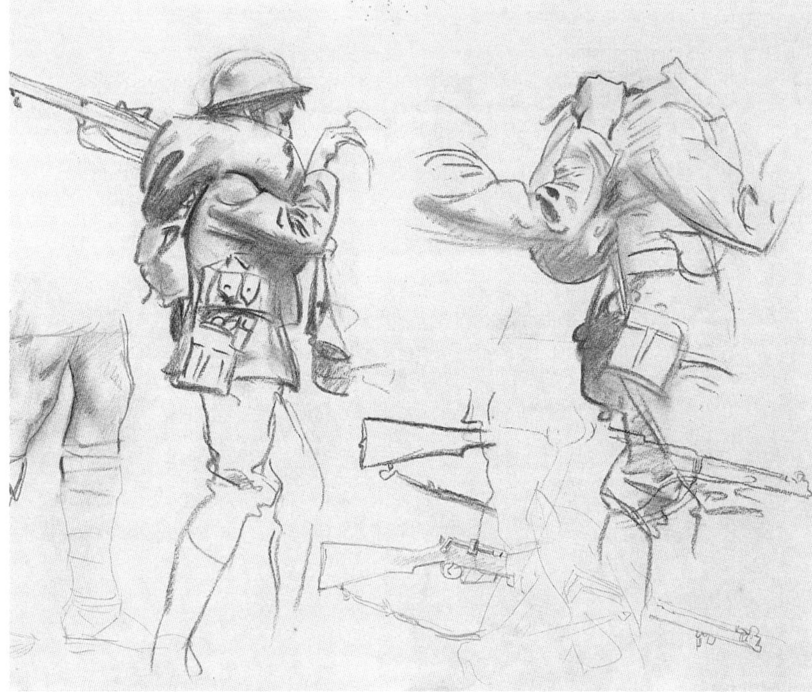

↑
John Singer Sargent, *Study for Gassed: studies of standing soldiers with rifles, c.*1918

PENCIL AND CHARCOAL ON PAPER

This charcoal drawing includes three images of rifles that relate to areas of the final oil painting. The more established study of the figure to the left, laden with kit and carrying his rifle over his shoulder, connects directly to the figure towards the back of the frieze-like line in the middle ground of *Gassed*.

In *Gassed*, Sargent's figures connect either by touch or kit. As in the line of blinded men linked by staffs in Bruegel's *The Parable of the Blind*, Sargent here uses a rifle to create another linkage. He wanted to create an unbroken chain from left to right across the visual line of the painting.

Exhibition at the Royal Academy in May 1919, the first after the Armistice. Critics tended to use the Summer Exhibition to assess the state of British art, offering both a chance to reflect and to prophesise about emerging trends. So soon after the war's end, the weight of expectation was heavy. As reviewer Claude Phillips put it in the *Daily Telegraph* on 3 May: 'We are at a moment of climax in the world's history and, not unnaturally, have expected it to be accompanied by a turning-point in the world's art.'[2]

Gassed occupied a pride of place spot in Gallery Three and created a central point of focus.[3] About half the paintings included in the Summer Exhibition addressed the subject of war and its aftermath. George Clausen's *Youth Mourning* – painted following the war death of Clausen's daughter's fiancé – was included. So was the large canvas of war artist Anna Airy, *A Shell Forge at a National Projectile Factory, Hackney Marshes*, which had already entered the IWM collection. Some writers, including Virginia Woolf, criticised the prescriptive – possibly even manipulative – emotional provocation of the works included in the Summer Exhibition that year, which she felt 'jabbed and stabbed, slashed and sliced for close on two hours'.[4] Others noted the uneasy rub between weighty war subjects and the more pedestrian pre-war sensibilities on display elsewhere, which raised questions about the role of large national art exhibitions in a post-war world. However, the exhibition was very popular, with over 200,000 people visiting during the three month run.[5] *The Morning Post* critic praised *Gassed* as the show's best work in subject and execution. He concluded that 'Art is of the greatest service to humanity when it commemorates noble deeds'.[6]

In December 1919 *Gassed* was included in a landmark loan exhibition entitled *The Nation's War Paintings and Other Records*, also held at the Royal Academy. The exhibition included many of the memorial paintings and sculptures created towards the end of the war under the aegis of the British War Memorials Committee (BWMC) as well as works made by other official war artists, including modernists such as brothers Paul Nash and John Nash, Stanley Spencer and CRW Nevinson. The exhibition was a triumph, running until February 1920, longer than planned due to public interest. It was credited as one of the most successful exhibitions ever to be staged at the Royal Academy and even with marking a new dawn for art in a civic context. As Sue Malvern has written, 'modern art had finally discovered a public function, and, as a consequence, a

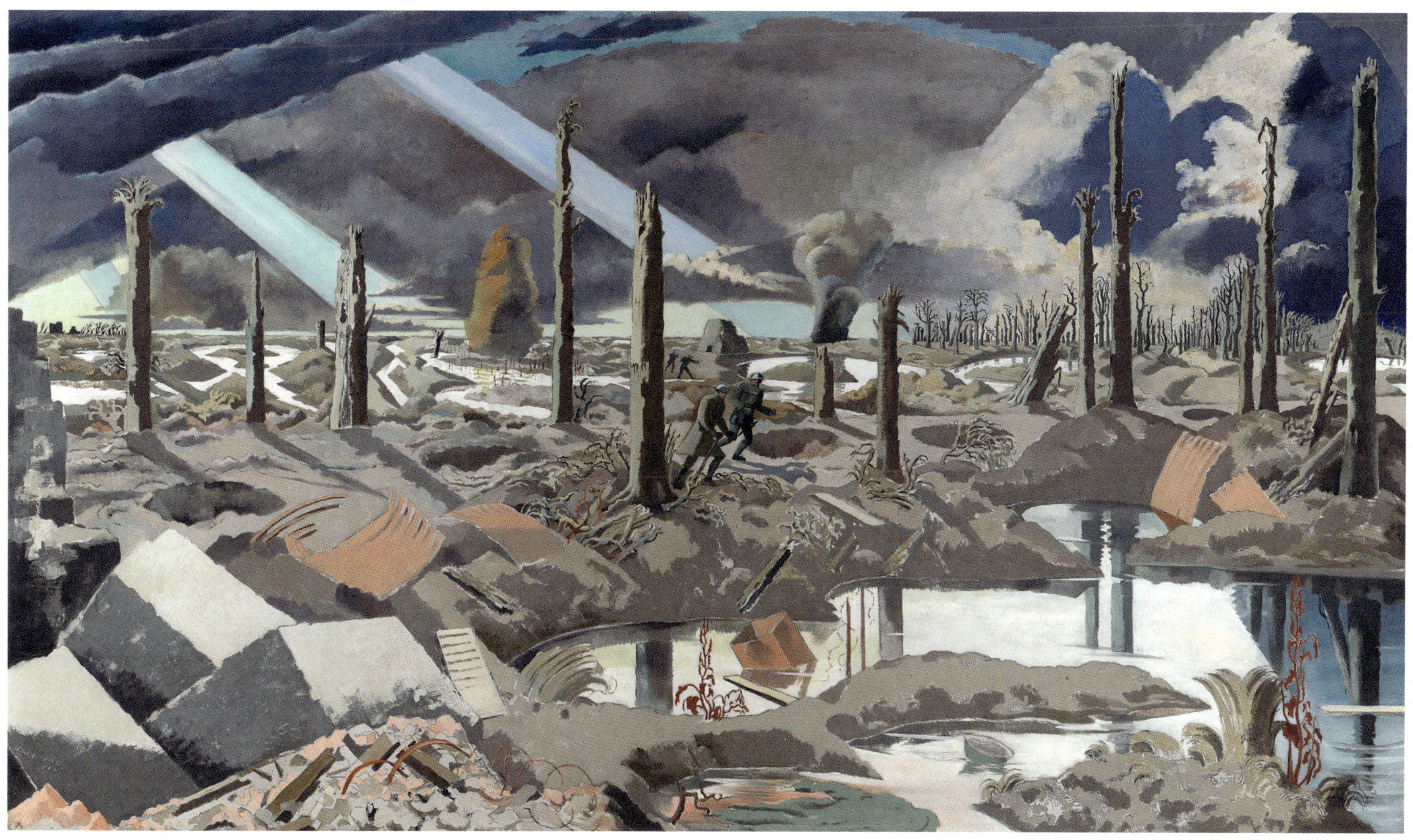

↑

Paul Nash, *The Menin Road,* 1919

OIL ON CANVAS

Young modernist artist Paul Nash received the commission for this work, originally titled *A Flanders Battlefield*, from the BWMC in April 1918. It depicts a devastated battlefield pocked with rain-filled shell-holes, flooded trenches and shattered trees, lit by unearthly beams of light from an apocalyptic sky.

Two figures pick their way along a tree-lined road punctuated by shell-holes. In the carnage of war, the trees are just stumps. The foreground is filled with concrete blocks, barbed wire and corrugated iron, while columns of mud from artillery fire rise up in the background. Through this landscape of war, Nash commented on the harsh new world order, in which everything has been rearranged.

On the painting's completion, Nash offered a description of the painting for the proposed Hall of Remembrance, though the project was never realised. He observed that 'The picture shows a tract of country near Gheluvelt village in the sinister district of "Tower Hamlets", perhaps the most dreaded and disastrous locality of any area in any of the theatres of War.'

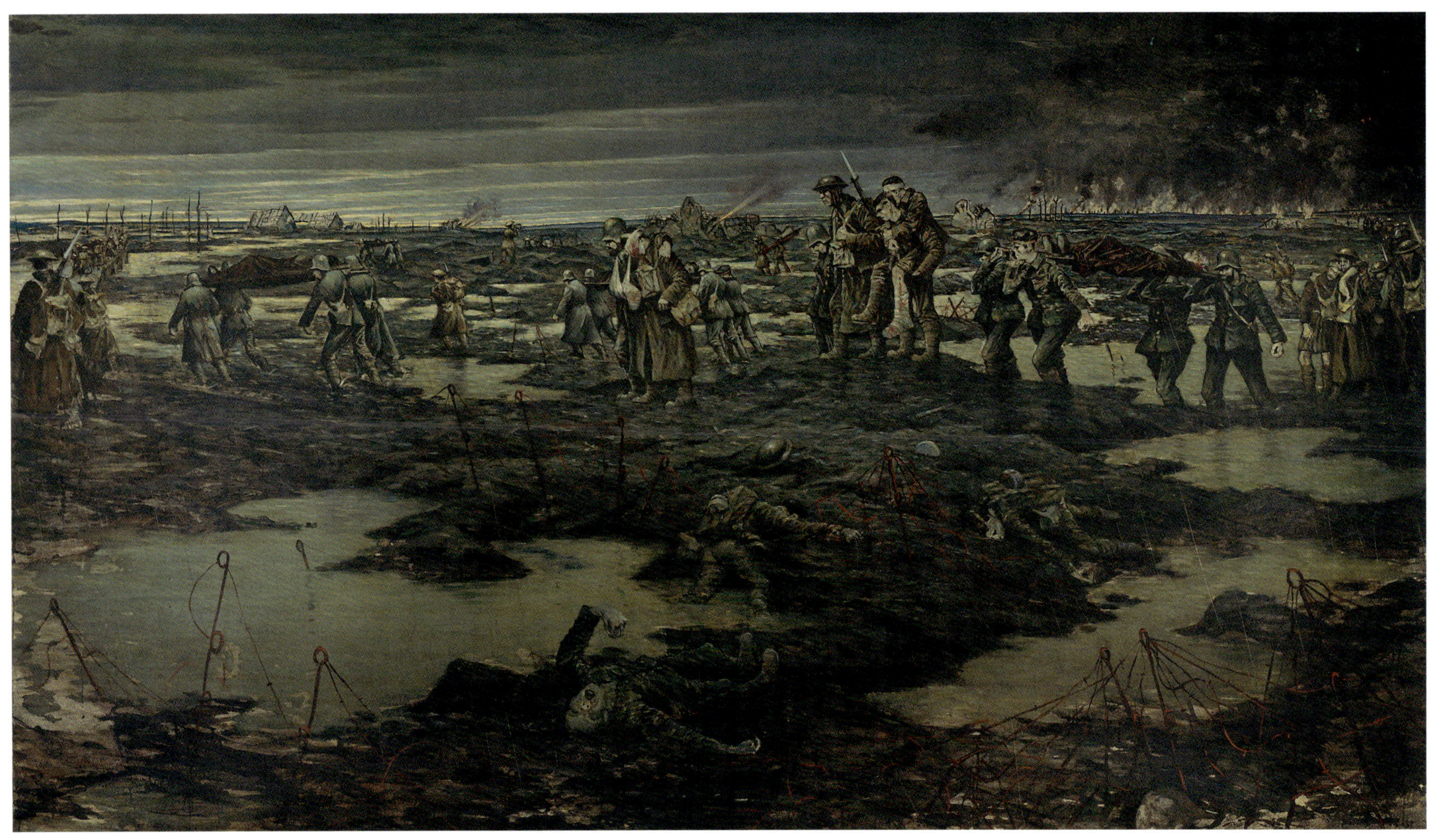

↑
Christopher Richard Wynne Nevinson,
***The Harvest of Battle,* 1919**
OIL ON CANVAS

Aged 29, CRW Nevinson was commissioned as part of the BWMC scheme in 1918, alongside John Singer Sargent. He described producing the sketches for this resultant work during a short trip to Passchendaele that year: 'We arrived at Ypres, and ... I wandered up towards the Salient and obtained notes and rough sketches for my painting'. Nevinson's painting provides a stark view of the carnage of war and reveals the BWMC's commitment to its authentic portrayal. In a letter to Alfred Yockney, the BWMC Secretary, he described the work as: 'A typical scene after an offensive at dawn. Walking wounded, prisoners and stretcher cases are making their way ... through water-logged country of Flanders. By now the Infantry have advanced ... only leaving the dead, mud and wire'.

Appointed an official war artist in 1917, Nevinson's war paintings are also informed by earlier service experiences. On the outbreak of the First World War in 1914, Nevinson, already known as a radical modernist artist, had volunteered for the Red Cross; he later served as an ambulance driver, stretcher bearer and hospital orderly before ill health forced his return to Britain. A fervent pacifist, he was deeply disturbed by his experiences, but they stimulated him artistically. He wrote in a newspaper article that 'All artists should go to the front to strengthen their art by a worship of physical and moral courage'.

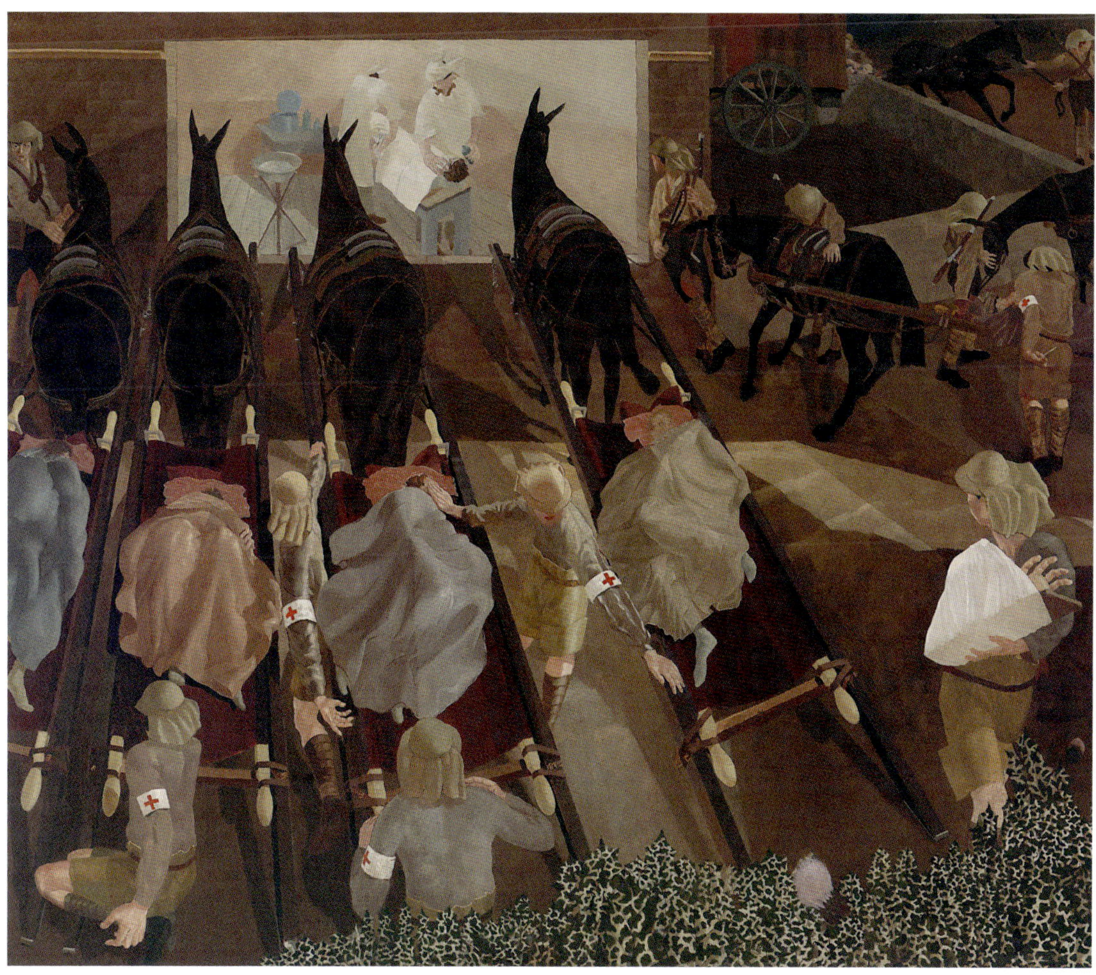

↑

Stanley Spencer, *Travoys Arriving with Wounded at a Dressing-Station at Smol, Macedonia, September, 1916*, 1919

OIL ON CANVAS

In April 1918, while serving in Macedonia, 26-year-old Stanley Spencer was asked by the BWMC to complete a commission, its suggested subject a religious service at the front. This is the resultant work – included, alongside *Gassed*, in an influential Royal Academy exhibition of war paintings in 1919. Spencer noted that in his painting he wanted to 'show God in the bare real things, in a limber wagon, in ravines, in fouling mule lines'.

This scene is based on Spencer's experiences with the 68th Field Ambulance, which he described in a letter to BWMC Secretary Alfred Yockney in August 1919: 'In the middle of September 1916 the 22nd Division made an attack on Machine Gun Hill ... During these nights the wounded passed through the dressing stations in a never-ending stream'. During Spencer's time at the front, he was stationed near the old Greek church depicted in the painting, to which casualties were brought on mule-drawn stretchers, or travoys.

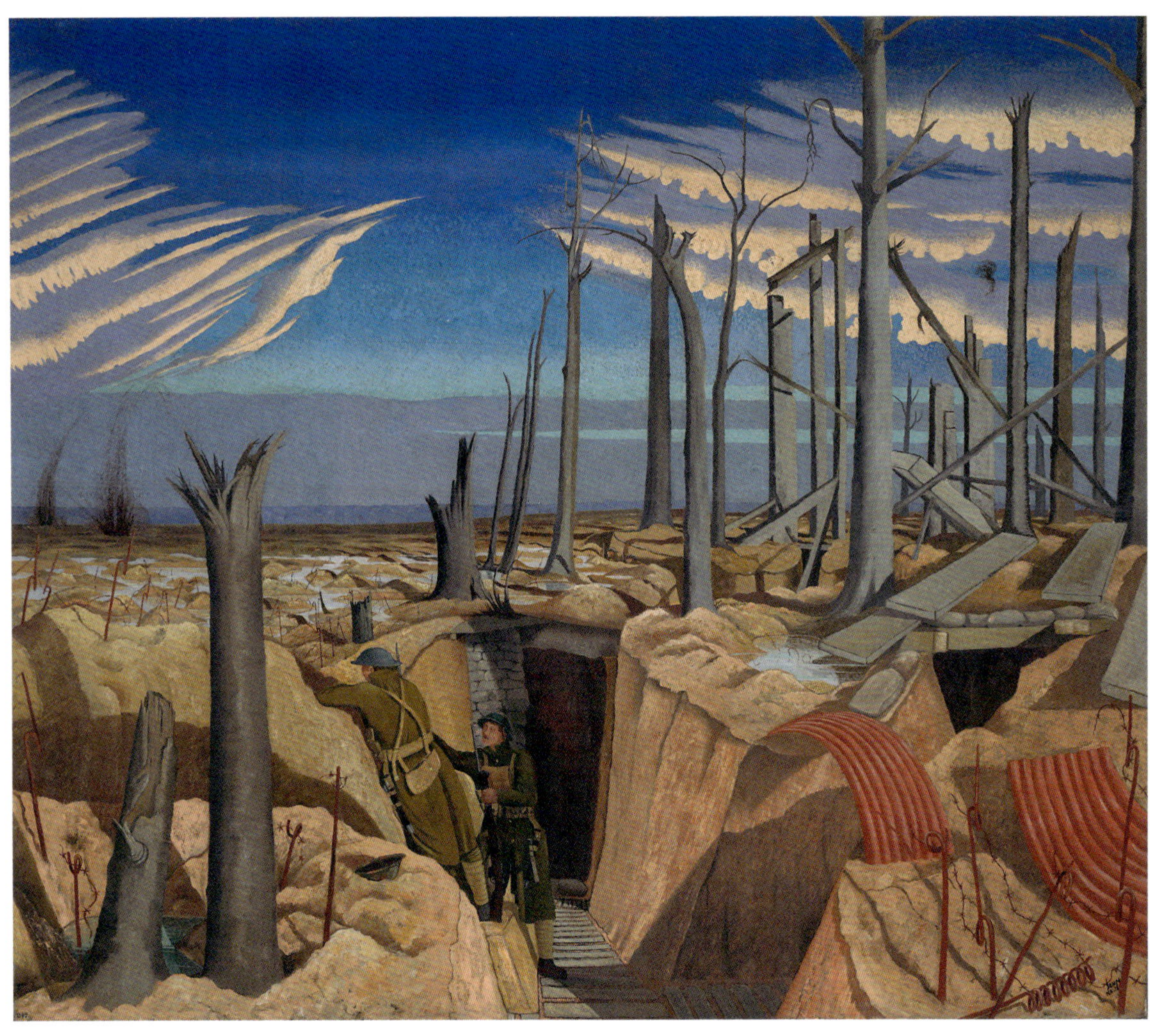

↑
John Nash, *Oppy Wood, 1917 – Evening,* 1918

OIL ON CANVAS

This scene includes a view down into a trench with duckboard paths leading to a dugout. Two infantrymen stand to the left of the dugout entrance, one of them standing on the fire-step to look over the parapet into no man's land.

Aged 25, John Nash was commissioned by the BWMC in 1918 as part of their plan to include soldier-artists. Among them were some of the most avant-garde British artists of the time, including the artist brothers John and Paul Nash, both of whom had seen service on the front line. Despite this, the initiators of the scheme conceived of it within a long-established tradition of artistic patronage, influenced by models from the Renaissance. It was intended that works produced as part of the memorial scheme would celebrate national ideals of bravery, sacrifice and heroism, with *Gassed* acting as the centrepiece; the works in the end came to IWM.

This work was relocated in August 1939 to a less vulnerable site outside London, in anticipation of bombing raids over the capital. IWM had been urged to activate its evacuation plan after it received a direct hit, but actually moved out only a small proportion of artworks. The inclusion of *Oppy Wood* on the list confirms its high cultural significance by the time of the Second World War, and the pre-eminent status of the modernist Nash brothers alongside canonical artists such as Sargent.

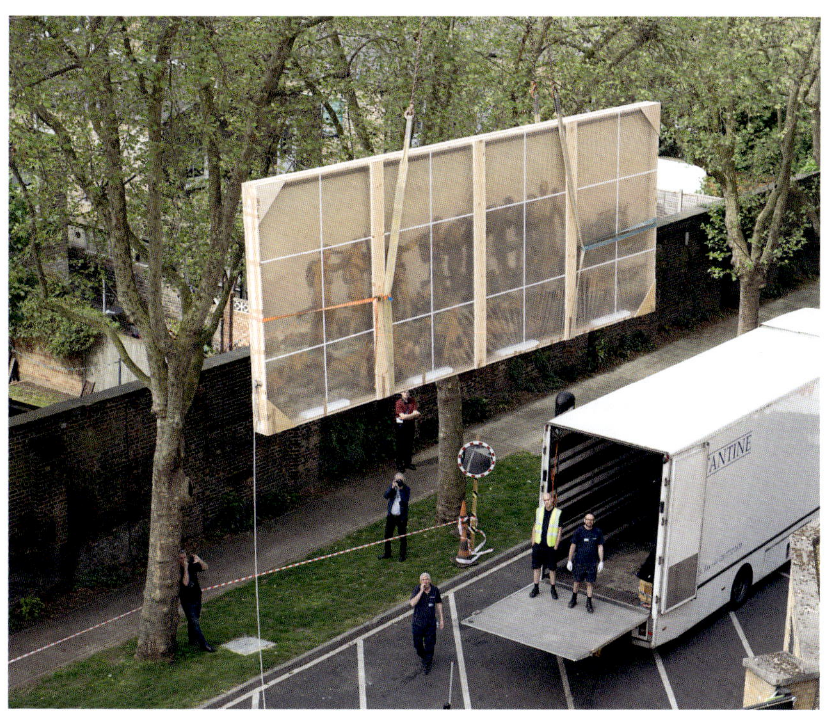

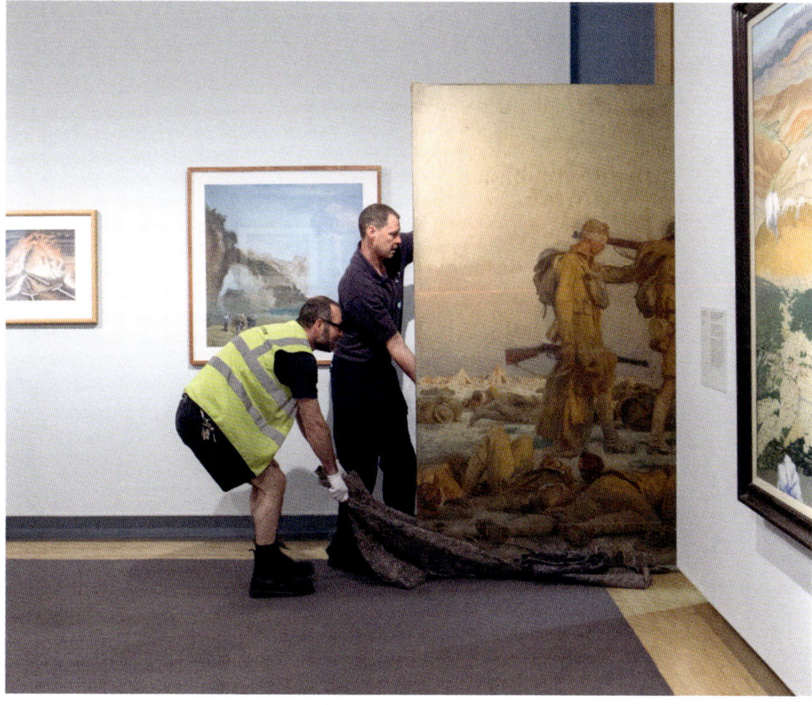

↑
Gassed moved by crane outside IWM London, 2016
In early November 2016 Constantine art handlers helped to move Sargent's monumental painting out of IWM London ahead of a tour of North America, which marked the centenary of America's involvement in the First World War. *Gassed* began its tour at the Pennsylvania Academy of Fine Arts (PAFA) where it was displayed as part of the exhibition *World War I and American Art.*

"new renaissance" had come about, based on a consensus eliminating the polarities and fractures in pre-war British art.'[7]

Since *Gassed* found its home at IWM, it has rarely been off display. Perhaps more than any other object, visitors to IWM London have expected to see the painting on public show, and it has mostly occupied dedicated gallery space here because of its monumental size. Despite the threat of bombing, the IWM galleries were largely kept intact during the Second World War. The only significant conservation intervention in the decades since *Gassed* was made took place in the 1970s, when the painting was removed to be cleaned and revarnished. It featured in tours to America in the 1990s and, most recently, as part of First World War Centenary exhibitions between 2016 and 2018. Material degradation of *Gassed* is surprisingly minimal despite its age – its size and special status have meant that movement, handling and material degradation have been minimised for the whole of its century-long life.

Ahead of its redisplay in the Blavatnik Art, Film and Photography Galleries, new conservation (including the methodical removal of

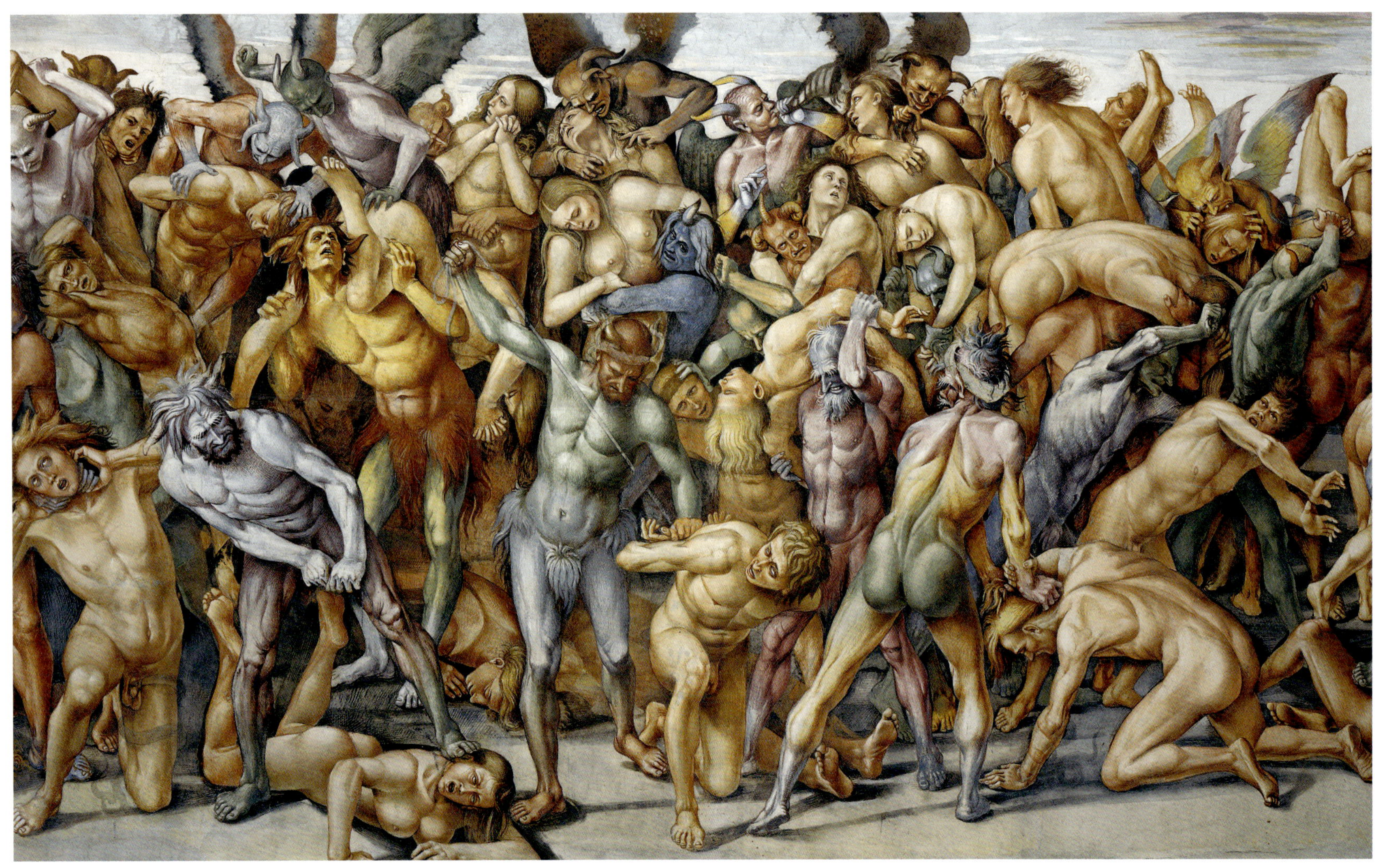

↑

Luca Signorelli, *The Damned, c.*1499–1502

FRESCO, CHAPEL OF SAN BRIZIO, ORVIETO CATHEDRAL

John Singer Sargent was acutely aware of his art-historical inheritance. As artists before him had done, he mined it for inspiration and a source of gravitas during the development of *Gassed*. One such touchstone was *The Damned*, part of a large Renaissance fresco cycle representing the events of the Apocalypse and Last Judgement, created for Orvieto Cathedral. Sargent's commission was likewise to take centre stage in a grand memorial hall – a new kind of cathedral for a new post-war world.

For *The Damned*, the artist Luca Signorelli produced a huge, writhing cast of muscular, nude figures – pushing, pulling, screaming and contorting as some exact judgement and others suffer physical punishment.

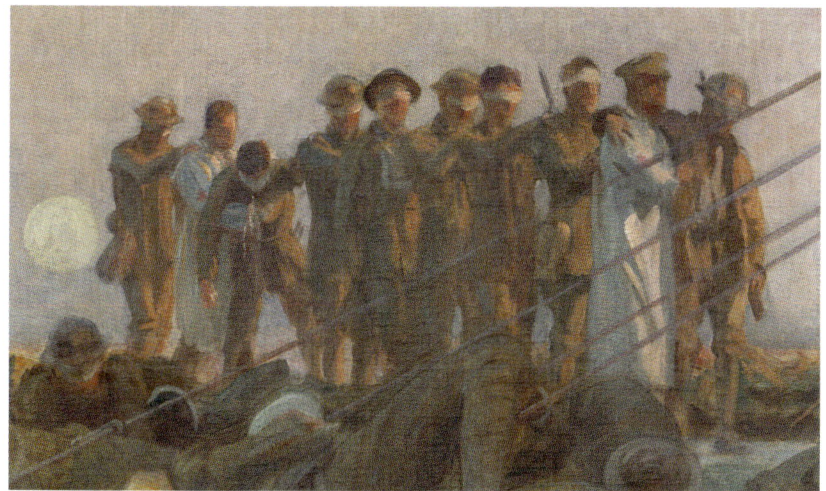

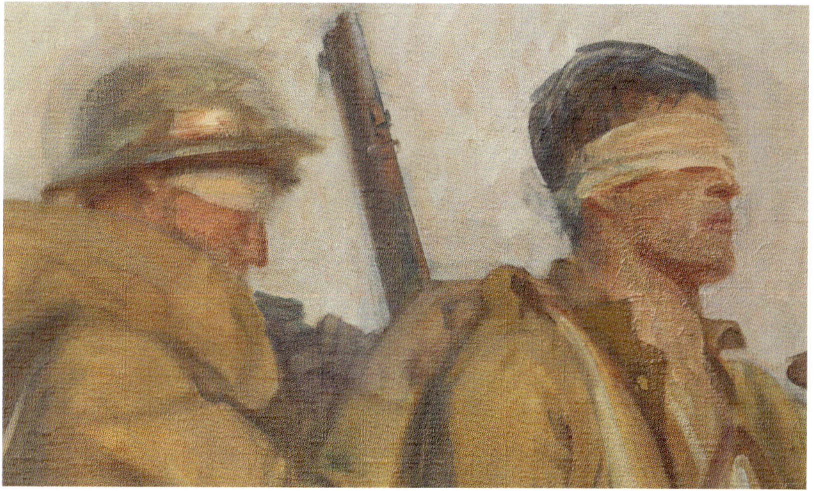

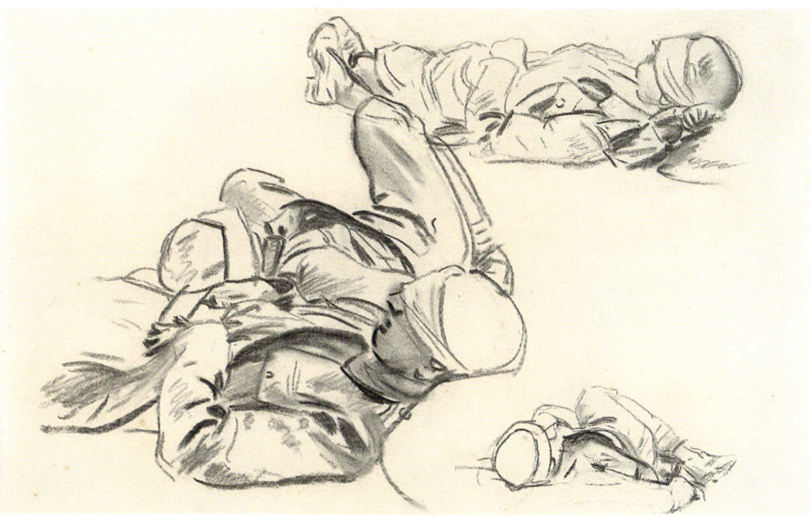

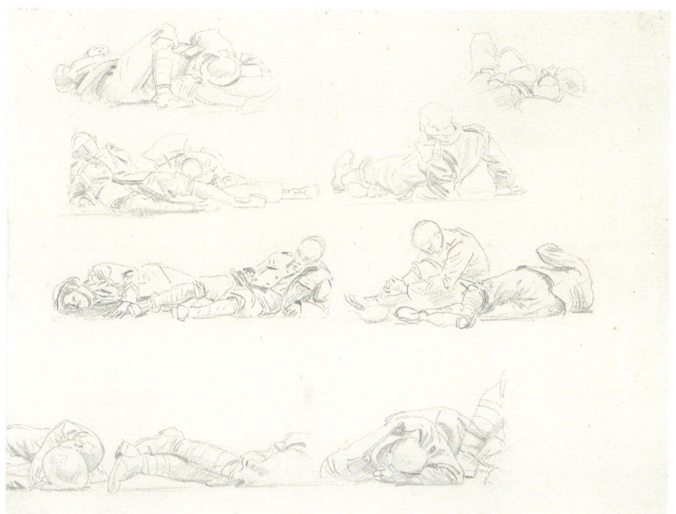

↑ ↗
Details of John Singer Sargent, *Gassed*, 1919
OIL ON CANVAS
Sargent was interested in quotation from art history. Signorelli's depiction of a mass of bodies influenced his development of the frieze of soldiers who move across *Gassed* from left to right, and of the pile of suffering gassed cases in the foreground. The interlocking of figures, through gesture, pose and touch, also refers to Signorelli's art historical precedent.

↑
John Singer Sargent, Study for *Gassed*: three studies of soldiers with bandaged heads, *c.*1918
CHARCOAL ON PAPER
In his preparatory studies, Sargent worked out the relationships between figures which he then transposed to the large canvas of *Gassed*. In approaching his task, he drew upon both his eyewitness experience and art historical traditions and motifs, including Signorelli's contorted and suffering figures.

↑
John Singer Sargent, Study for *Gassed*: eight studies of soldiers, *c.*1918
PENCIL ON PAPER
Sargent's careful observations of reclining men suffering from the effects of gas exposure on the front line informed the group of interlocked bodies in the foreground of *Gassed*. His eyewitness experience informed the artist's ambition to create an epic with 'masses of men'.

the now-discoloured 1970s varnish) and cutting-edge 3D, infrared and multispectral imaging have revealed the clarity and economy of Sargent's painting once again. In the painting there is a notable absence of reworking, a fluidity in the treatment of light and colour alongside careful modelling of form and structure: everything has its place. As Richard Ormond has described it, in *Gassed* we can see Sargent's, 'skill in putting one brush stroke next to another of exactly the right value without confusing the two ... He could replicate the surface texture of things, seen under specific conditions of light, in a few swift strokes.'[8]

The recent conservation work has confirmed the exceptional physical qualities of the painting and restored its legibility. *Gassed* is an art-historically infused interpretation of a real event. Sargent drew directly on his eyewitness experience for the fragments of modern war in *Gassed* – strewn bodies, signs of chemical warfare, men blinded and vomiting, medical personnel in action, a football match in red and blue shirts, duckboards and guy ropes. At the same time the line of soldiers, each arm to shoulder and groping for footing, creates an allegorical frieze across the middle ground of the painting, alluding to images of religious procession from the Renaissance and classical antiquity. Sargent drew together classical and modern references which can together be understood as a grand, timeless narrative of human suffering and human redemption.

JOHN SINGER SARGENT – WAR ARTIST

Sargent was 62 years old when he travelled to France and Belgium as an official war artist and painted *Gassed*. In some ways he was an unusual choice. He was known as a prolific and highly successful portraitist, particularly of the upper echelons of society, among whom he moved easily. This work had made him a wealthy man and had certainly impacted his reputation. While Sargent had experimental periods and was engaged particularly with Impressionism (he described a close affinity with Claude Monet, whom he met in 1876), by the time of the First World War his style had been fairly consistent for some decades, somewhere between traditional and progressive.[9]

Sargent was born in Florence in 1856 to affluent American parents who had moved to Europe with the aim of embracing its culture. The family never returned to America, nor did they establish a permanent home. Sargent lived a privileged, itinerant young life with his parents and siblings (he was especially close to his mother and sister Emily). He spent time travelling, studying and working in Europe and found success in Paris before settling in London in 1886.

In London Sargent exhibited at the Royal Academy. He became a founding member of the New English Art Club, established by a group of painters who were dissatisfied with entrenched art world academia and 'united in their art sympathies' towards the looser, fresher avant-garde.[10] He was elected a Royal Academician in 1897, testament to his status in Britain by that point. Though a private character in some ways, he 'hobnobbed with patricians' and 'enjoyed the power of a public figure'. Sargent could demand in-person visits from sitters at his studio at 33 Tite Street, Chelsea; his prestige was such that his American patrons duly made the journey.[11] Most of the artist's clients were aristocrats and wealthy plutocrats for whom he created portraits reflecting status and advantage at 1,000 guineas a time (about £100,000 today). His work rate was formidable. Between 1900 and 1907 he painted 15 to 25 portraits a year and devoted energy to working *en plein air*, which would remain important to Sargent until his death. During a trip to America in 1903 he painted 20 portraits, including one of President Theodore Roosevelt.[12]

Perhaps because of his nomadic background and rarefied circumstances, at the outbreak of the First World War Sargent remained 'disarmingly naïve about events taking place around him'.[13] The war did not really touch him until his niece was killed in a German bombardment on Paris in 1918. In the period between 1915 and 1917 he was in America, occupied with commissioned work in Boston. Perhaps restless (in 1907 he had declared himself 'sick and tired of portrait painting'), Sargent did not clamour for a war artist commission, something altogether outside what he had previously attempted. As early as October 1916 he confided to his future biographer Evan Charteris: 'would I have the nerve to look, not to speak of painting? I have never seen anything the least horrible – outside my studio'.[14]

THE WAR ARTIST EXPERIENCE

Several attempts were made to convince Sargent to take a war artist commission. He eventually agreed in June 1918, providing a passport photograph held now in the IWM archives *(opposite)*, and was posted to France. He travelled with surgeon and fellow artist Henry Tonks,

→
Letter to John Singer Sargent, 12 June 1918
→→
Ministry of Information instruction from Colonel Galloway, 10 June 1918

Plans were made for John Singer Sargent and fellow artist Henry Tonks to travel to France in early July 1918. Tonks, a trained surgeon, was 'so well-known to the Medical Profession a conducting officer will not be necessary, nor need he wear a uniform'. The situation for Sargent was different. However, these BWMC minutes instructed that he be permitted to move around, accompanied by a military officer, in order that he could obtain the sketches he needed for a 'picture of British and American troops co-operating together'. Sargent supplied the photograph below for his passport.

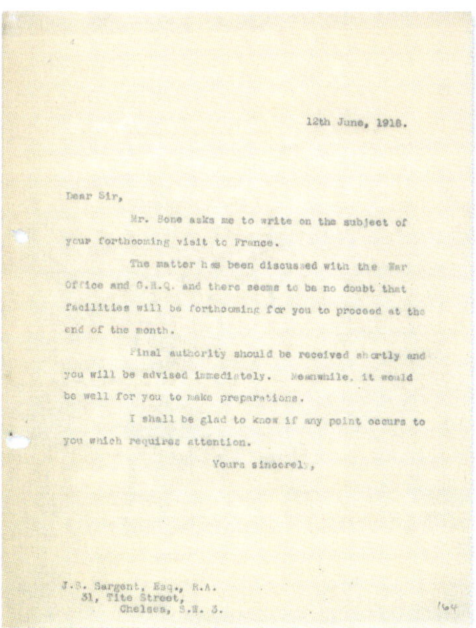

12th June, 1918.

Dear Sir,

Mr. Bone asks me to write on the subject of your forthcoming visit to France.

The matter has been discussed with the War Office and G.H.Q. and there seems to be no doubt that facilities will be forthcoming for you to proceed at the end of the month.

Final authority should be received shortly and you will be advised immediately. Meanwhile, it would be well for you to make preparations.

I shall be glad to know if any point occurs to you which requires attention.

Yours sincerely,

J.S. Sargent, Esq., R.A.
31, Tite Street,
Chelsea, S.W. 3.

164

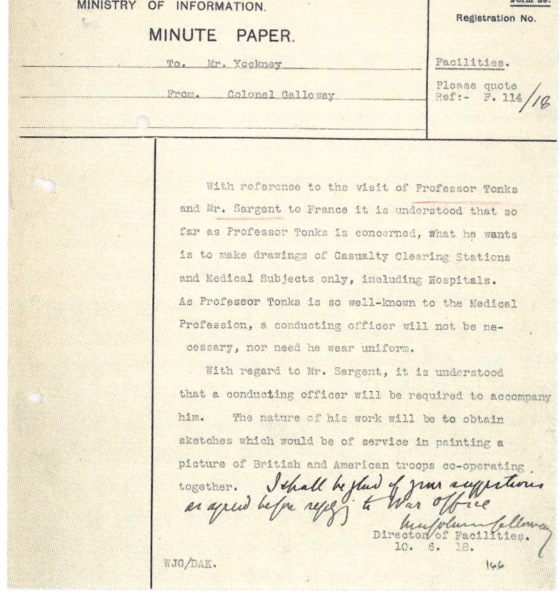

MINISTRY OF INFORMATION.

MINUTE PAPER.

Form 29.

Registration No.

To. Mr. Yockney

From. Colonel Galloway

Facilities.

Please quote Ref:- F. 114/18

With reference to the visit of Professor Tonks and Mr. Sargent to France it is understood that so far as Professor Tonks is concerned, what he wants is to make drawings of Casualty Clearing Stations and Medical Subjects only, including Hospitals. As Professor Tonks is so well-known to the Medical Profession, a conducting officer will not be necessary, nor need he wear uniform.

With regard to Mr. Sargent, it is understood that a conducting officer will be required to accompany him. The nature of his work will be to obtain sketches which would be of service in painting a picture of British and American troops co-operating together. I shall be glad of your suggestions as agreed before replying to War Office

Director of Facilities.
10. 6. 18.

WJG/DAK.

166

→
Letter from Alfred Yockney to John Singer Sargent, 26 April 1918

Alfred Yockney, former editor of *The Art Journal* and Secretary of the BWMC, wrote to John Singer Sargent in April 1918. The letter invited Sargent to become part of the BWMC war art scheme, and laid out the terms and scope of a possible commission: 'It is thought very strongly that you would be among the first painters to undertake a composition. I am instructed accordingly by the Committee to make the proposition for you and to express the hope that you will be able execute such a work. The subject the Committee have in mind is one which would suggest the fusion of British and American forces, but if you would like to name an alternative, I am sure that the Committee would hear your views.'

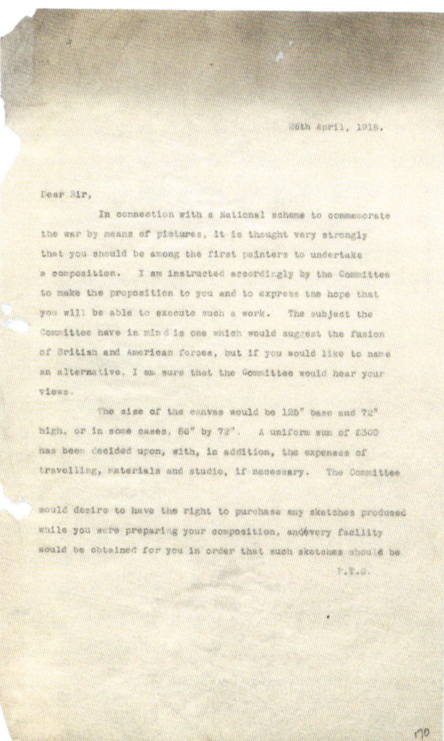

26th April, 1918.

Dear Sir,

In connection with a National scheme to commemorate the war by means of pictures, it is thought very strongly that you should be among the first painters to undertake a composition. I am instructed accordingly by the Committee to make the proposition to you and to express the hope that you will be able to execute such a work. The subject the Committee have in mind is one which would suggest the fusion of British and American forces, but if you would like to name an alternative, I am sure that the Committee would hear your views.

The size of the canvas would be 125" base and 72" high, or in some cases, 86" by 72". A uniform sum of £300 has been decided upon, with, in addition, the expenses of travelling, materials and studio, if necessary. The Committee would desire to have the right to purchase any sketches produced while you were preparing your composition, and every facility would be obtained for you in order that such sketches should be

P.T.O.

170

→→
Photographic portrait of John Singer Sargent, *c.*1918

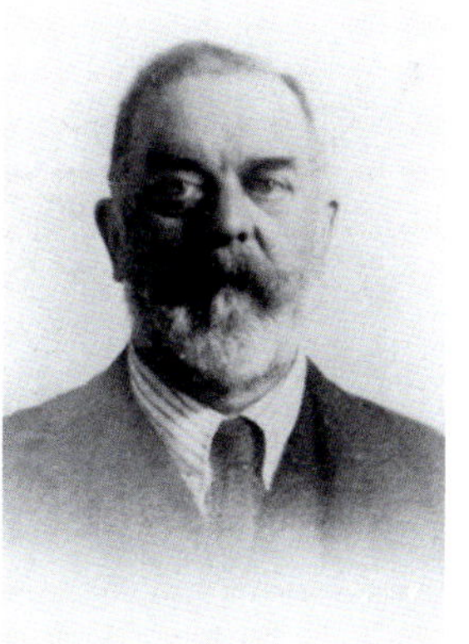

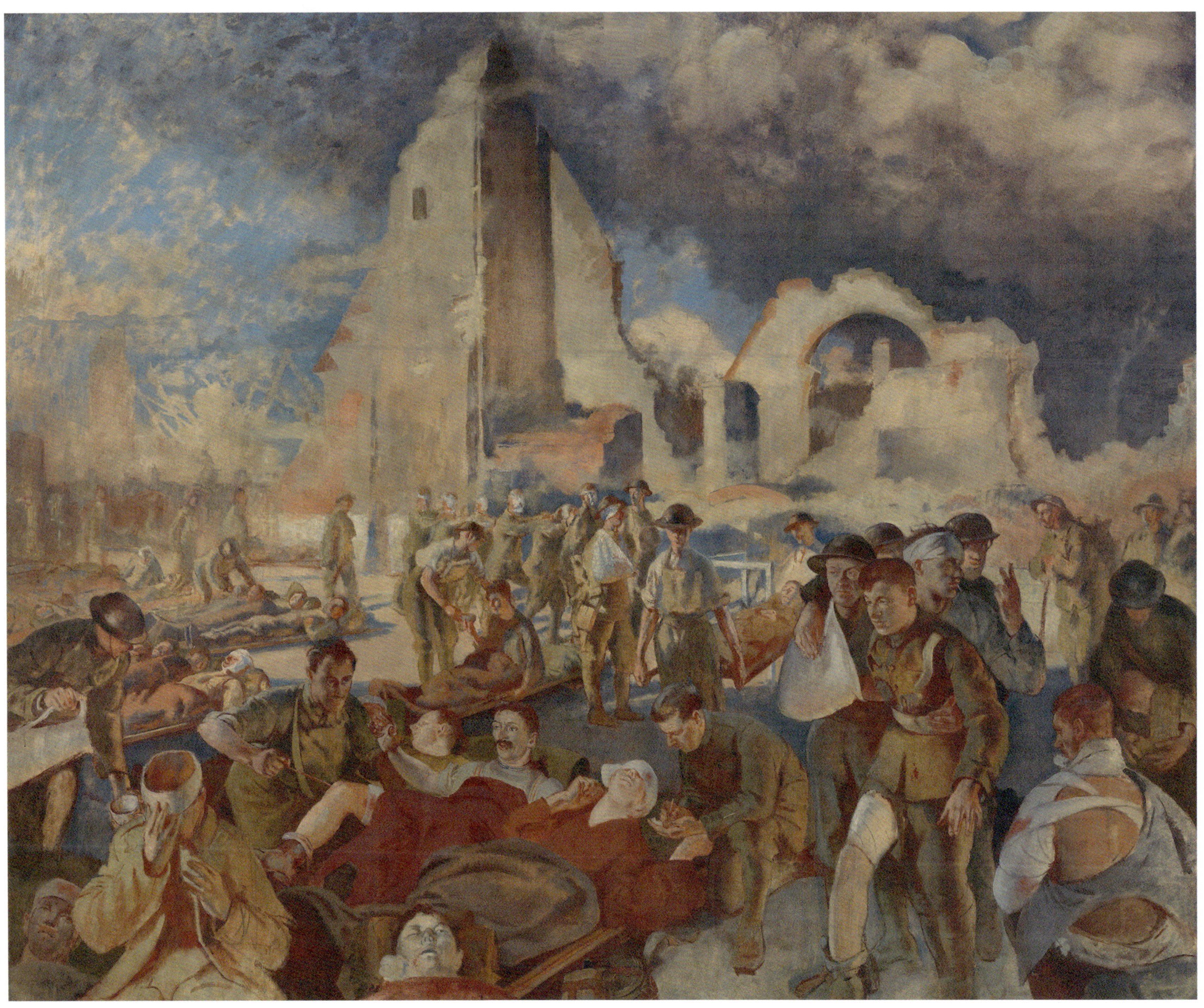

←

Henry Tonks, *An Advanced Dressing Station in France*, 1918

OIL ON CANVAS

Artist Henry Tonks was drawing master at the Slade School of Art. Before the First World War he taught a new generation of bright young modernists there, including Paul Nash, Stanley Spencer and CRW Nevinson.

Tonks had previously trained as a surgeon. He resumed his medical career during the First World War, serving with the Royal Army Medical Corps, then became a war artist in 1918. Commissioned like John Singer Sargent by the BWMC, he travelled to the Western Front with him. Tonks's commission was to depict an advanced medical dressing station and this canvas was the resultant work.

An Advanced Dressing Station in France captures a scene amid a German offensive in 1918, within which Tonks exploits his medical expertise to showcase a wide range of injuries, treatments and field dressings.

and both wrote often and richly of their experiences. His friend Evan Charteris noted that Sargent was 'excited and interested' before departure. He observed that the artist 'regarded the question of his outfit very seriously, and 31, Tite Street soon became littered with boots, belts and khaki'.

Sargent's official commission came from the government's BWMC, a downstream committee of the Ministry of Information; he had also received a personal invitation from David Lloyd George, then Prime Minister. Lloyd George described the BWMC commission as 'a work of great and lasting service to the nation' and encouraged Sargent to accept it. The Committee comprised some influential people including Charles Masterman, the former head of propaganda, and Muirhead Bone, the first official war artist. Bone had travelled to the front in 1916 and had conceived impressive plans for the character of the BWMC's scheme as a 'highly original and transgressive enterprise'.[15] As Sue Malvern has described, its aim was to 'assemble a significant contemporary collection representative of "the great artistic expression of the day" … as a memorial to the war'.[16] It was to encompass established art world figures and new modernists, some of whom had seen service directly.

Given the grand plans for the form, scale and conception of the works, the Committee landed on Uccello's *Battle of San Romano* in the National Gallery, measuring 6 by 10 feet (over 3 metres wide), as a good benchmark for the commissioned artists. In addition, three 'supersized' works would be commissioned from Sargent, Augustus John and William Orpen, with the suggested themes of Anglo-American, Anglo-French and Anglo-Italian co-operation respectively. These were just suggestions: artists commissioned as part of the scheme were afforded relative freedom and were not strictly allocated topics on which to focus.[17] The BWMC had drawn up a list of Western Front and home front topics deemed suitable, but many were not translated into practice. Some artists, including young modernists who had themselves served on the front line, were asked to make suggestions of their own. It was understood that the first priority was to consult potential artists and give them licence. However, the scheme did require that all artists visit the Western Front and gain eyewitness experience so that the works 'would provide authentic testimony and … serve the purposes of remembrance'.[18]

Under such a weighty brief, Sargent grappled with finding a subject for his commission for some time in France. It is likely that he was underprepared for what he might encounter and he clearly wanted to do the task justice. Early on he had considered what it meant to paint an epic fit for the remembrance brief, and probably felt the weight of art history on his shoulders. Indeed, Sargent had considered Luca Signorelli's *The Damned* frescoes for Orvieto Cathedral, begun in 1499, as the exemplary treatment of a swirling mass of bodies. He corresponded back and forth with Charteris and the administrators of the scheme regarding the BWMC's expectations of the work's theme and scale:

> The Ministry of Information expects an epic – and how can one do an epic without masses of men? Excepting at night I have only seen three fine subjects with masses of men – one a harrowing

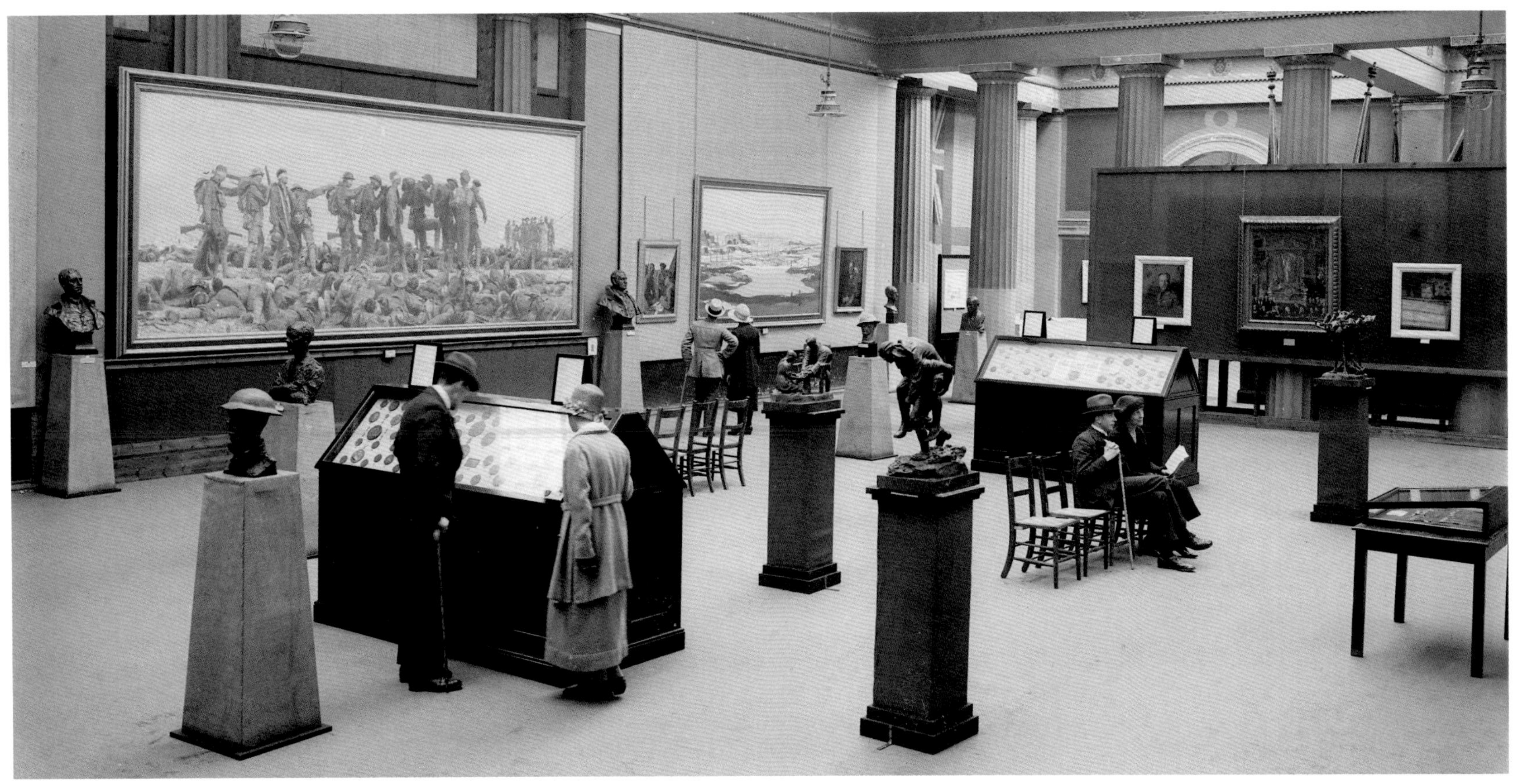

↑
An art room at the Imperial War Museum, Crystal Palace, *c.*1920
The Imperial War Museum (IWM) opened its first 'permanent' exhibition at Crystal Palace on 9 June 1920 after three years of temporary measures. Charles ffoulkes, Curator and Secretary of the museum from 1917 to 1933, was responsible for establishing the collections and overseeing displays.

> sight, a field full of gassed and blindfolded men – another a train of trucks packed with 'chair a cannon' – and another frequent sight, a big road encumbered with troops and traffic. I daresay the latter, combining English and Americans, is the best thing to do.[19]

Then came a breakthrough. In a letter to BWMC Secretary Alfred Yockney, Tonks described the context for *Gassed* after the men had witnessed the aftermath of a gas attack on 21 August 1918:

> After tea we heard that on the Doullens Road at the Corps dressing station at le Bac-du-Sud there were a good many gassed cases, so we went there. The dressing station was situated on the road and consisted of a number of huts and a few tents. Gassed cases kept

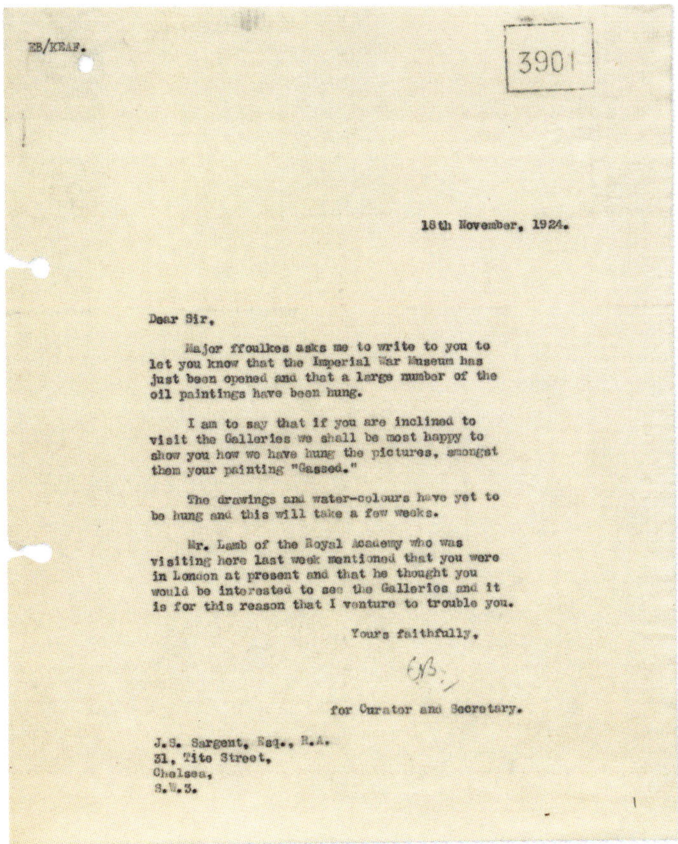

EB/KEAF.

3901

18th November, 1924.

Dear Sir,

Major ffoulkes asks me to write to you to let you know that the Imperial War Museum has just been opened and that a large number of the oil paintings have been hung.

I am to say that if you are inclined to visit the Galleries we shall be most happy to show you how we have hung the pictures, amongst them your painting "Gassed."

The drawings and water-colours have yet to be hung and this will take a few weeks.

Mr. Lamb of the Royal Academy who was visiting here last week mentioned that you were in London at present and that he thought you would be interested to see the Galleries and it is for this reason that I venture to trouble you.

Yours faithfully,

EB.

for Curator and Secretary.

J.S. Sargent, Esq., R.A.
31, Tite Street,
Chelsea,
S.W.3.

↑

Letter from Ernest Blaikley to John Singer Sargent, 18 November 1924

By 1924 four million people had visited the galleries of the IWM in Crystal Palace, but the Palace's glass structure made the environment too unstable for collections in the longer term. It became clear that the museum would have to find a new location and radically downsize. The new venue offered was the Western Galleries at the Imperial Institute in South Kensington. This letter inviting Sargent for a tour of the new spaces makes clear that BWMC oil paintings – including *Gassed* – were a priority for display.

> coming in, led along in parties of about six just as Sargent has depicted them, by an orderly. They sat or lay down on the grass. There must have been several hundred, evidently suffering a great deal, chiefly I fancy from their eyes, which were covered up by a piece of lint … Sargent was very struck by the scene and immediately made a lot of notes.[20]

In *Gassed* we can see a central tension between a personal, eyewitness account of a specific time and place and a more timeless interpretation of the magnitude and impact of the war; between representing an individual fragment and saying something significant about the whole. Evan Charteris described how Sargent gave 'a spiritual value to realism, and dignity and solemnity to the facts'.[21] It is the dichotomous artistic challenge set by the BWMC that makes the paintings that arose from the scheme – *Gassed* in particular – all the more exceptional and compelling.

IWM

By the time it was wound up in 1919 the BWMC scheme had produced 17 history paintings including the monumental *Gassed*, 12 smaller canvasses and two sculptural reliefs. It had involved 31 artists, some on a one-off basis, others employed continuously for up to ten months. Sargent was paid £600 for *Gassed*, double the rate of other artists because of the supersized scale of the work.

In the development of the BWMC scheme there was always an expectation that the works could and would be seen together – and the artists also imagined an audience in the execution of their commissions. In 1918 Muirhead Bone wrote a paper about an eventual Hall of Remembrance; in it he imagined a noble space sited on Richmond Hill surrounded by gardens that would house the canvasses and sculptures, and even incorporate music. The committee went as far as engaging the services of leading architect Charles Holden, although he was busy elsewhere and provided just a single sketch for the imagined Hall. In the event, disagreement about the purpose and future of the BWMC meant that the resultant war art collection was brought under the aegis of a newly formed Pictorial Propaganda Committee. When the promise of funding from the Treasury fell through, this new committee quickly abandoned the Hall of Remembrance. Instead it designated the IWM, which had

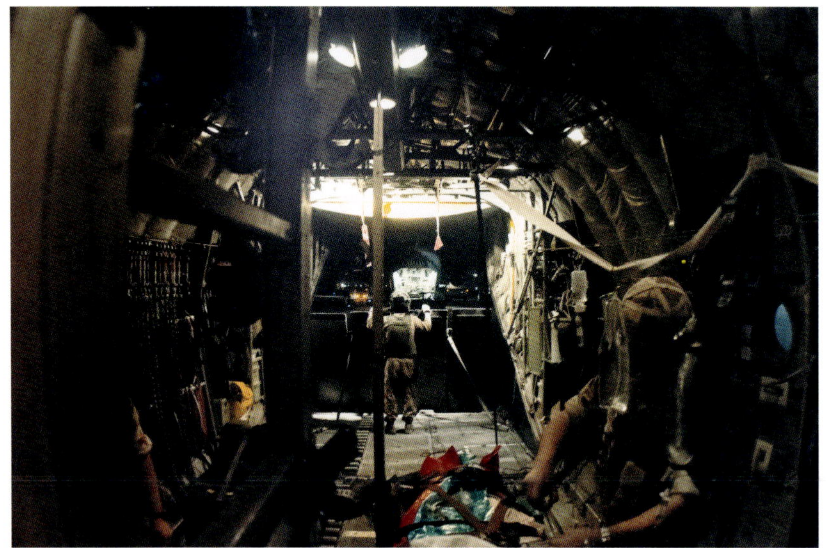

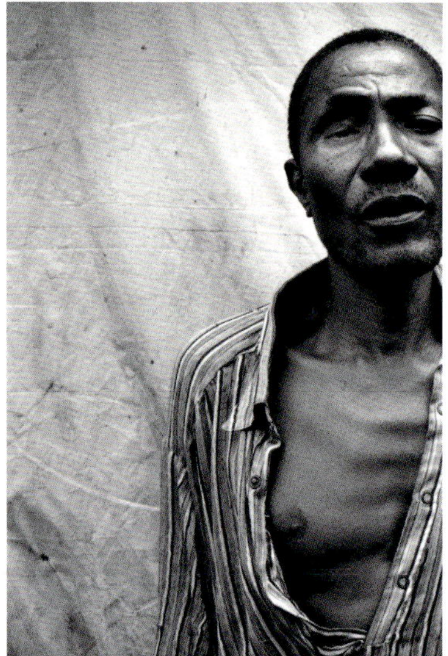

←←
David Cotterrell, *Gateway II*, 2009
C-TYPE PRINT ON ALUMINIUM

←
Tim Hetherington,
***War Blind* series, 1999–2004**
DIGITAL PHOTOGRAPH FROM
35MM FILM BASE NEGATIVE

been founded in 1917, as the permanent home for the commissioned paintings. *Gassed* has been a cornerstone of IWM's art collection ever since.

The BWMC scheme left a rich art historical legacy. Its operation and focus on artists, as well as the resonance with audiences of the paintings that arose from it, provided a benchmark for Kenneth Clark and others in the setup of the much bigger War Artists' Advisory Committee scheme during the Second World War. The works commissioned by the BWMC – and produced within the wider First World War artist scheme – proved that artists could provide a vital service during conflict and that modern art could do more than survive in the most extreme context: it could thrive.

Gassed returns to display at IWM London in new galleries dedicated to IWM's art, film and photography collections. It will occupy a new wall built to house the painting in a thematic section considering the effects of war on the mind and body. On display nearby, David Cotterrell's *Gateway II* photographs consider similar themes. Produced after the artist was commissioned to observe medics at Camp Bastion, Afghanistan, they depict unconscious young bodies being airlifted to receive further treatment and rehabilitation elsewhere – medics take them somewhere out of shot, just as in *Gassed*. Also nearby, works from Tim Hetherington's *War Blind* portrait series offer another consideration of sight loss because of war. Made during civil war in Sierra Leone, they engage directly with the theme of vision; light and shadow play across the surface of the images.

For the first time works made under the BWMC scheme will exist in sustained dialogue with other parts of IWM's visual media collections, and with works produced in disparate times and places of conflict. The works displayed together speak to the importance of war artists across the last century in defining how we think and feel about conflict – and the continued relevance of First World War works of art as powerful testimony to the human cost of war.

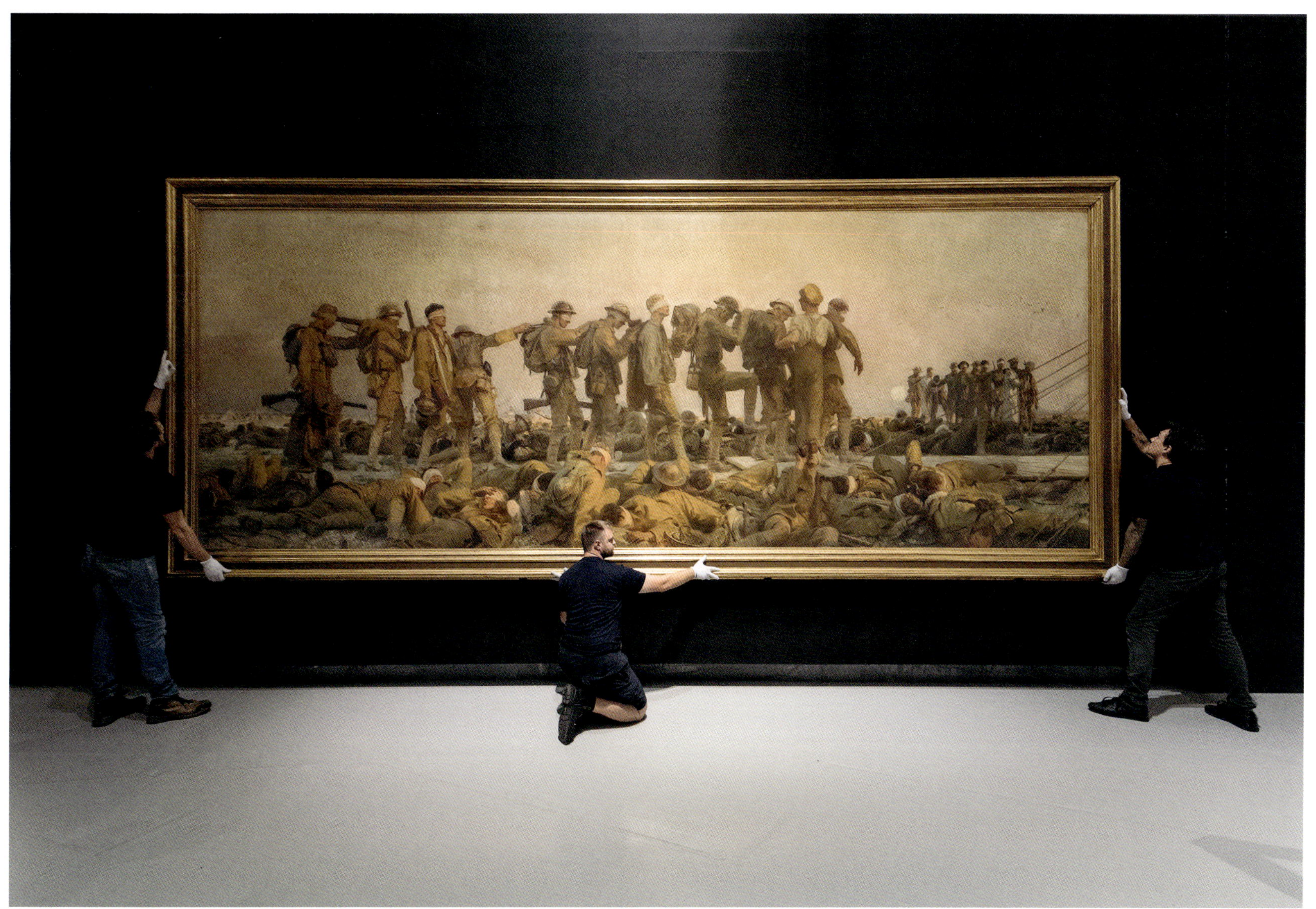

↑
Installation of *Gassed* at IWM North, 2018
Gassed was displayed at IWM North in Salford from July 2018 to February 2019 in an exhibition entitled *Lest We Forget?* Included in the exhibition were the paintings once destined for the Hall of Remembrance that was never built, among them *Gassed*.

TIMELINE

1914–1916

28 July 1914
Outbreak of the First World War: Austria declares war on Serbia. The war then spreads to Germany, Russia and France.

4 August 1914
Britain enters the conflict, declaring war on Germany when it invades Belgium

22 April 1915
At Ypres, Germany launches the first gas attack on the Western Front, inflicting significant Allied casualties

16 August 1916
Muirhead Bone is appointed the first official war artist; arrives in France at the height of the Somme offensive

1918

6 March 1918
First meeting of the government's British War Memorials Committee (BWMC), set up to commission works of art for a memorial to the First World War

29 March 1918
Sargent's niece, Rose-Marie Ormond, is killed when a German shell strikes the church of Saint-Gervais, Paris. Sargent receives the news in Pustertal in Italy.

26 April 1918
Letter from Alfred Yockney, Secretary of the BWMC, invites Sargent to become a war artist as part of the scheme

16 May 1918
Letter from the British Prime Minister David Lloyd George urges Sargent to accept the BWMC commission

18 June 1918
Memorandum from BWMC confirms Sargent's commission on the proposed theme of Anglo-American co-operation

2 July 1918
Sargent and Tonks travel to France, spending time with troops near Arras and later at Ypres

21 August 1918
Sargent and Tonks witness the aftermath of a gas attack at Bac-du-Sud, on the Arras–Doullens road

11 September 1918
Sargent writes to Major Arthur Lee, British military censor in France of paintings by official British war artists, asking to extend his stay in France for a few more weeks

late September 1918
Sargent contracts influenza and spends a week in hospital near Roisel

11 November 1918
Armistice signed; hostilities in Western Europe cease

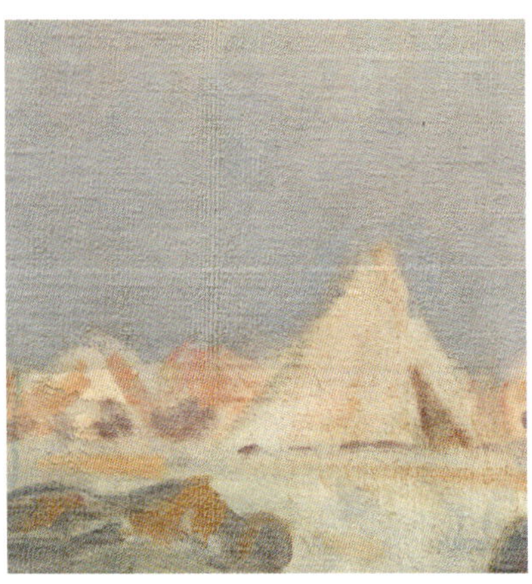

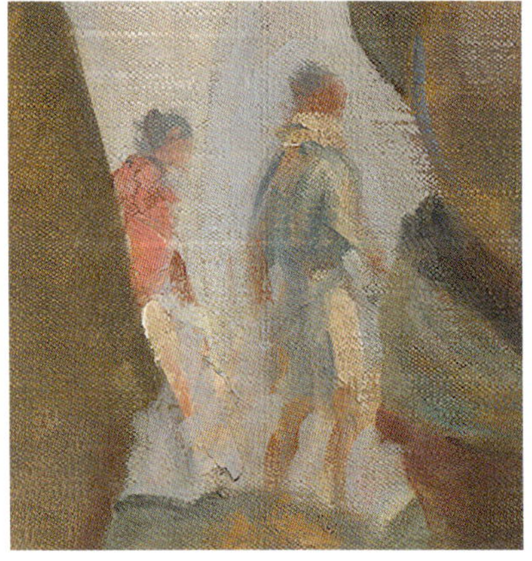

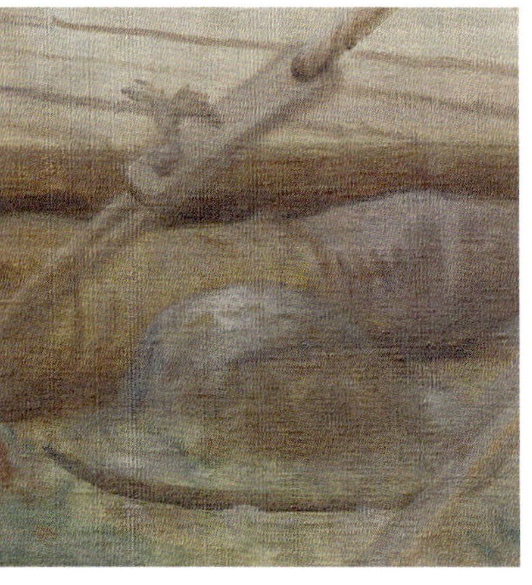

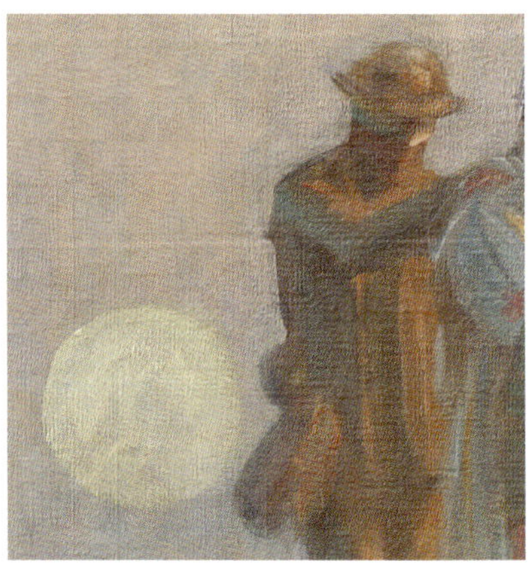

1919

March 1919
Back in London, Sargent completes the monumental oil painting *Gassed* from preparatory sketches made at the front. On completion, the work enters the IWM collection with the other works from the BWMC scheme. In all IWM collects around 4,000 paintings, sculptures and drawings related to the First World War.

5 May 1919
Gassed is included in the Summer Exhibition at the Royal Academy and is voted Picture of the Year

12 December 1919
Gassed becomes the only supersized BWMC painting to be included in an exhibition of the war art collection at the Royal Academy

1920–1936

9 June 1920
IWM's first 'permanent' exhibition at Crystal Palace opens, following three years of temporary displays and storage in various places; *Gassed* has pride of place

11 November 1924
Gassed is displayed at IWM's new premises at South Kensington

14 April 1925
Sargent dies in London, aged 69

1936
IWM's new museum premises in the former Bethlem Royal Hospital, Lambeth, include six art gallery rooms, with space dedicated to *Gassed*. The work becomes an audience favourite.

1999–2023

1999
Gassed tours North America for a series of retrospective exhibitions

2014
Gassed occupies its own room in IWM's *Truth and Memory* exhibition, the largest exhibition of British First World War art for almost 100 years

4 November 2016
Gassed begins an international tour to North America as part of First World War Centenary commemorations

27 July 2018
Gassed included as part of *Lest We Forget?* exhibition at IWM North, alongside other BWMC commissions

Dec 2022
Significant conservation analysis and work is begun on *Gassed* and its frame in preparation for new display at IWM London

3 July 2023
Gassed installed in brand new spaces at IWM London

10 November 2023
Gassed returns to display in newly reopened Blavatnik Art, Film and Photography Galleries at IWM London

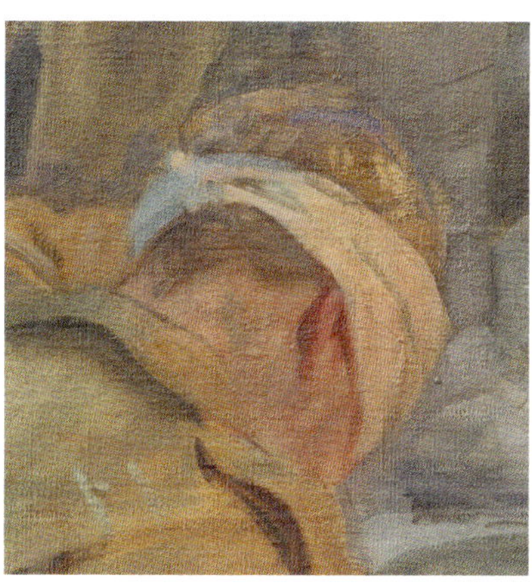

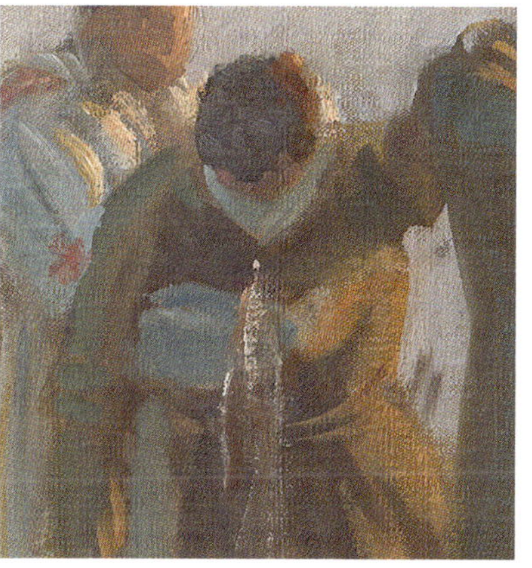

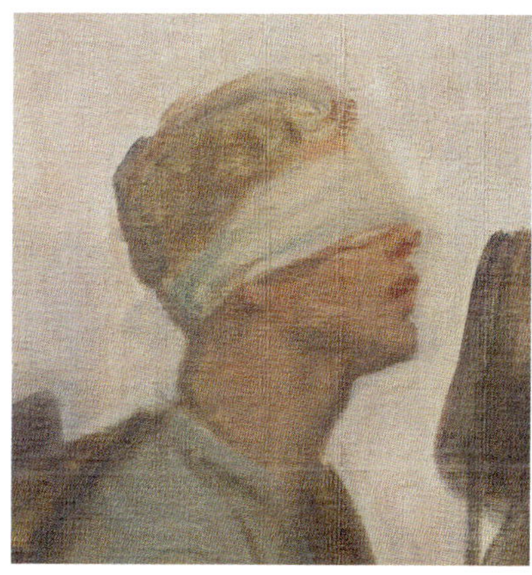

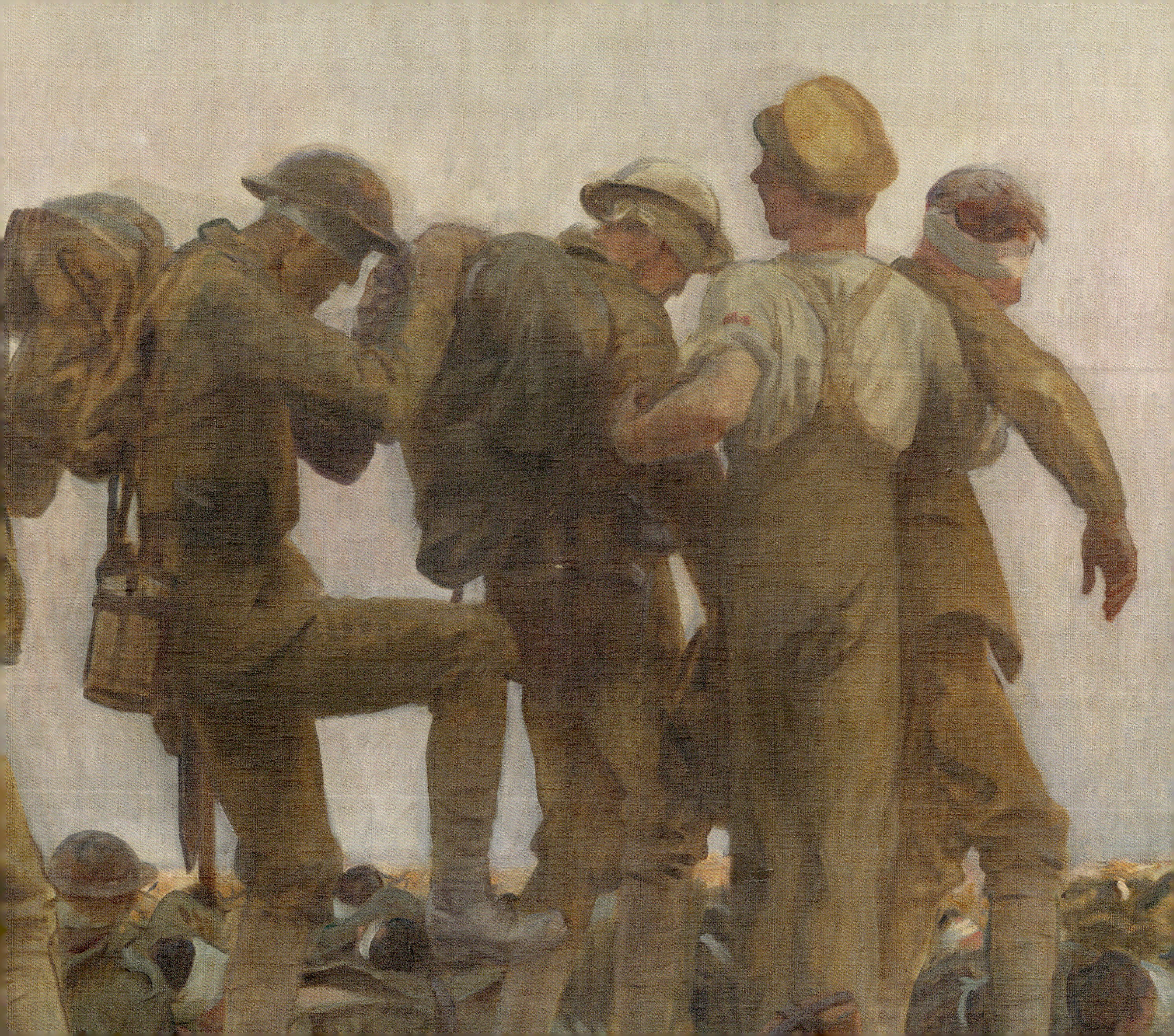

THE CREATION AND DISPLAY OF *GASSED*

By the time John Singer Sargent was commissioned by the government's British War Memorials Committee (BWMC) in 1918, the experience of war had already yielded some very significant works of art. Individuals including the first official war artist Muirhead Bone (sent to the Western Front in May 1916) had been lobbying the government for some time about the value and role of artists in documenting the experiences of the First World War. The artists included both traditional, establishment figures and new modernists, mostly educated at the Slade. In 1918 Sargent's commission and place in the wider war artist scheme was precisely defined. His work would be destined for a specially built gallery designed to act as a space for public and personal commemoration; the works featured in such a space would reflect ideals such as sacrifice, solidarity and bravery. Known as the Hall of Remembrance, the gallery was due to house the selection of works produced for the BWMC scheme, which by the time it was wound up consisted of 29 paintings as well as two large sculptural reliefs.

→
British War Memorials Committee memorandum, 18 June, 1918
The British War Memorials Committee (BWMC) was the initiative of Lord Beaverbrook, who was appointed first minister in the newly created Ministry of Information in February 1918. He established the Committee within the Ministry along lines similar to a Canadian scheme that he had previously overseen, filling it with influential cultural figures. The BWMC was the first example of British state patronage of modern art in the twentieth century; progressive for its time, it offered artists relative freedom of expression. The memorandum notes that 'Mr Sargent said he would like to see not only disembarcations *[sic]* and camp scenes, but also the sore, rugged side of war – the life in the trenches, the return of the men from the firing line and the real thing in regard to warfare. Lord Beaverbrook undertook that all possible facilities should be secured'.

→→
Letter from David Lloyd George to John Singer Sargent, 16 May 1918
David Lloyd George, prime minister at the time, urged Sargent to accept the war artist commission in this letter. To convince Sargent, he stressed the importance of the task at hand, commenting 'it is hoped that they will be handed down to posterity as a series of immortal works'. He added 'I write to support the suggestion made by the British War Memorials Committee that you should execute one of these large paintings, the subject being, I understand, one in which British and American troops are engaged in unison. If you will undertake this task you will be doing a work of great and lasting service to the nation.'

The proposition made to the artists engaged under the BWMC scheme was specific and unique. The scheme required them to visit the front, giving primary importance to the idea of immediate, eyewitness testimony. However, the artists were also conscious of their duty to provide a lasting record and memorial for future generations. As the prime minister David Lloyd George put it to Sargent (in a letter contained in the IWM War Artist Archive), 'If you will undertake this task, you will be doing a work of great and lasting service to the nation'. The artists were by the nature of the scheme encouraged to be reflective, to use hindsight, to recapitulate and underline. They were being asked to create a new form of history painting – a work of a religious, allegorical or moral message – in a cultural context in which genre still mattered and would be the benchmark against which art was judged. Yet at the same time new ideas had started to undermine long-standing tenets of art practice and art criticism, precipitated further by the experience of war.

Given the weight of the task, it is no wonder that Sargent hesitated. Traceable too in the IWM War Artist Archive letters and memos,

BRITISH WAR MEMORIALS COMMITTEE.

MEMORANDUM. Tuesday 18th June, 1918.

Mr. John S. Sargent R.A., and Professor Henry Tonks called to-day. I introduced them to Colonel Galloway, who is making arrangements for Passports and it was fixed that these artists should proceed to France on July 2nd.

Afterwards I took Mr. Sargent and Mr. Tonks to Lord Beaverbrook, who welcomed them and thanked Mr. Sargent especially for undertaking to paint a picture for the nation. Mr. Sargent said he would like to see not only disembarcations and camp scenes but the more rugged side of the war - the life in the trenches, the return of men from the firing line and the real thing in regard to warfare. Lord Beaverbrook undertook that all possible facilities should be secured.

156

COPY. 16th. May 1918.

Dear Mr. Sargent,

You have heard through Mr. Muirhead Bone and Professor Tonks that it is proposed to commemorate the War with a number of great paintings. These pictures will be preserved in a Memorial Gallery in London, and it is hoped that they will be handed down to posterity as a series of immortal works.

I write to support the suggestion made by the British War Memorials Committee that you should execute one of these large paintings, the subject being, I understand, one in which British and American troops are engaged in unison. If you will undertake this task you will be doing a work of great and lasting service to the nation.

Yours sincerely,

(Sgd). D. Lloyd George.

John S.Sargent, Esq., R.A.

168

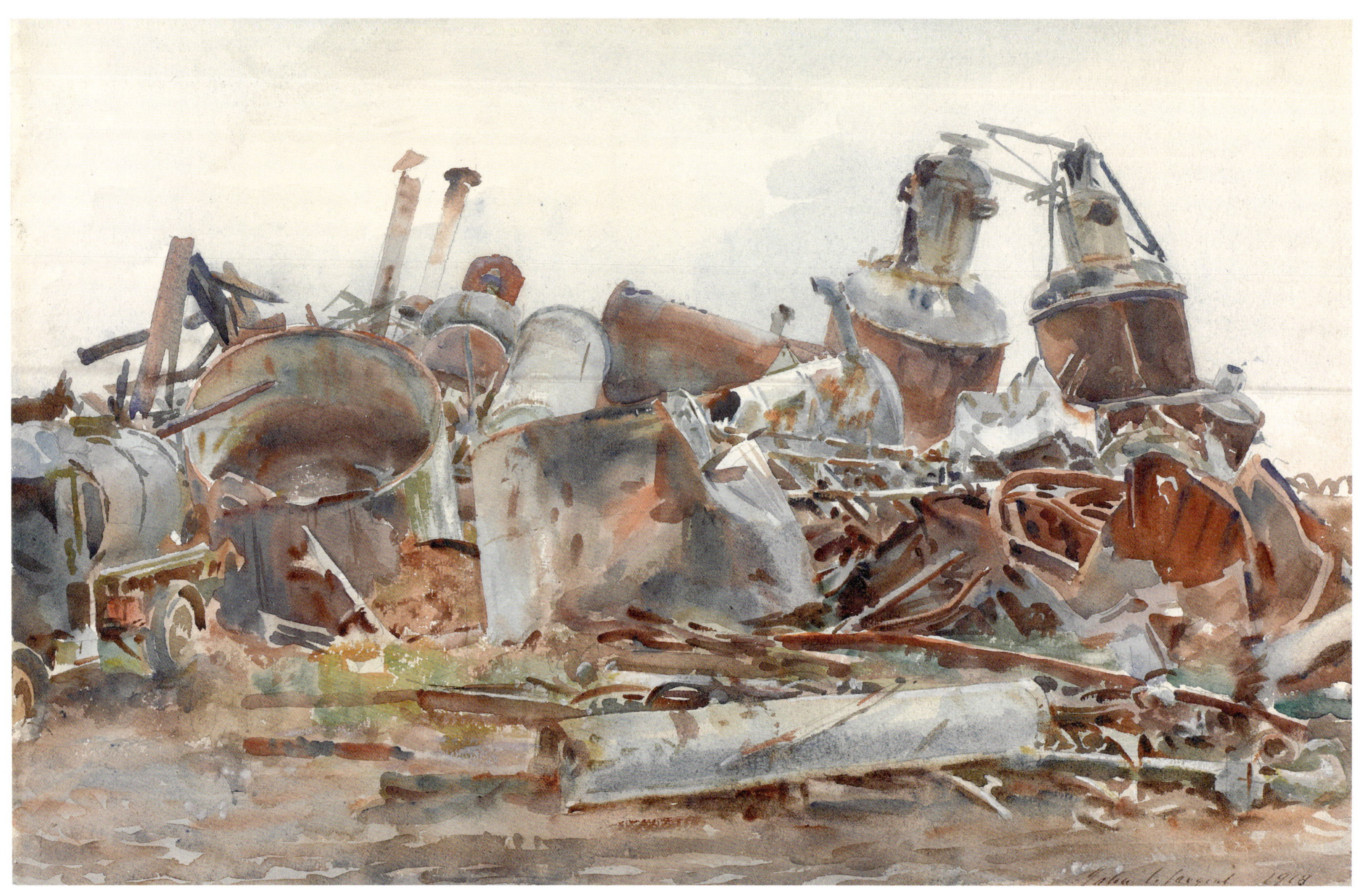

←

John Singer Sargent,
***A Wrecked Sugar Refinery,* c.1918**

WATERCOLOUR ON PAPER

On arrival in France, Sargent moved around, capturing the effects of war before settling on his subject for *Gassed*. Sargent brought his Impressionistic understanding of colour and light to this close observation of war wreckage. In this watercolour, the sugar refinery has become a useless pile of twisted metal and rusty drums. The pieces of debris are now relics of a former industrial power, rendered useless by the weaponry of modern war.

illustrated and explored in the following pages, is his initial equivocation, and his concerns throughout the process once he had accepted his commission. Sargent brought with him pre-eminent status and standing – the committee had recognised the primacy of the artist's voice in achieving ambitions for the scheme. It provided relative freedom in the official framework, appreciating the different approaches that individuals would take. To assist this, the committee also acted as a sounding board while artists worked out their plans, encouraging a collective troubleshooting through regular correspondence with commissioned artists.

Sargent had other precedents in mind, as well as the need to represent events for posterity as they unfolded around him. Following his thematic steer from the committee to work on 'British and American troops … engaged in unison', Renaissance artists Pieter Bruegel the Elder and Luca Signorelli provided a classical framework for quotation, their works exemplifying how to represent groups of human bodies under medical and combat tension. Sargent had made use of this heritage in a mural cycle for the Boston Public Library, a commission that had occupied him on and off since 1895 and was to continue alongside his BWMC commission until 1919. The committee's desire to construct a timeless memorial to the war still unfolding around them would have also encouraged a sense of a much longer human – and artistic – trajectory, and Sargent probably expected to face a similar proposition when he started to gather material for his BWMC commission. However, his arrival at the front in July 1918 brought a different perspective to the task. Sargent struggled to reconcile

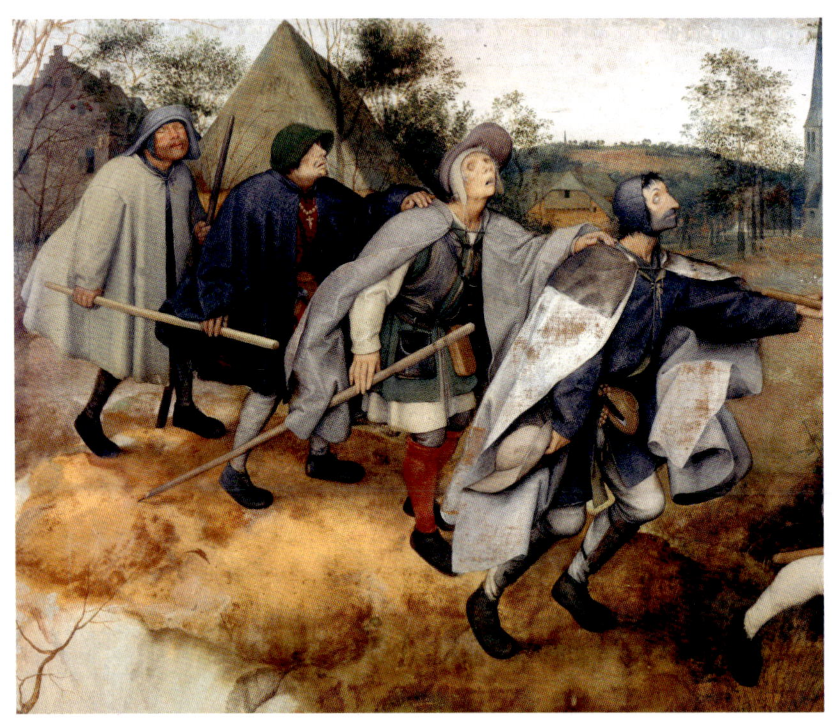

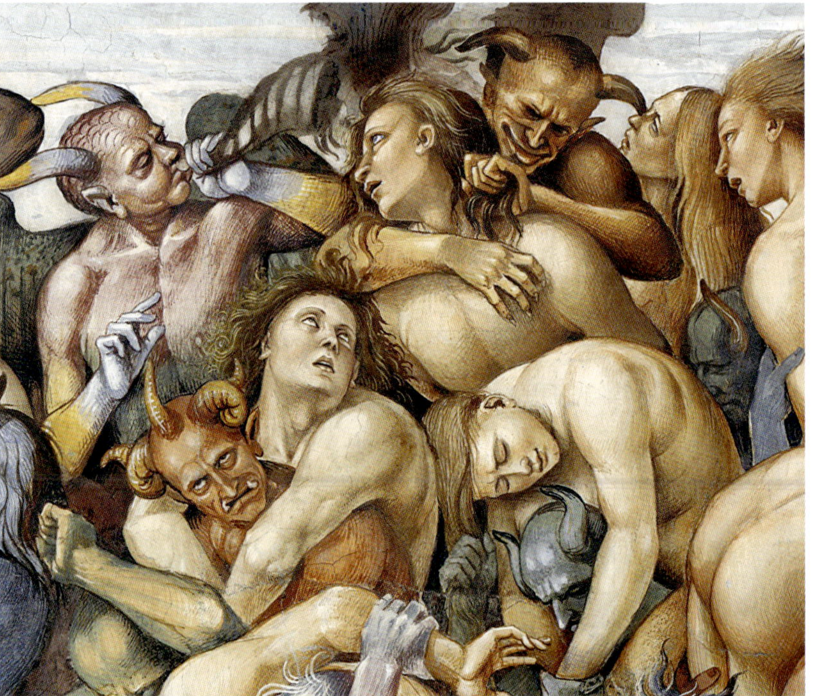

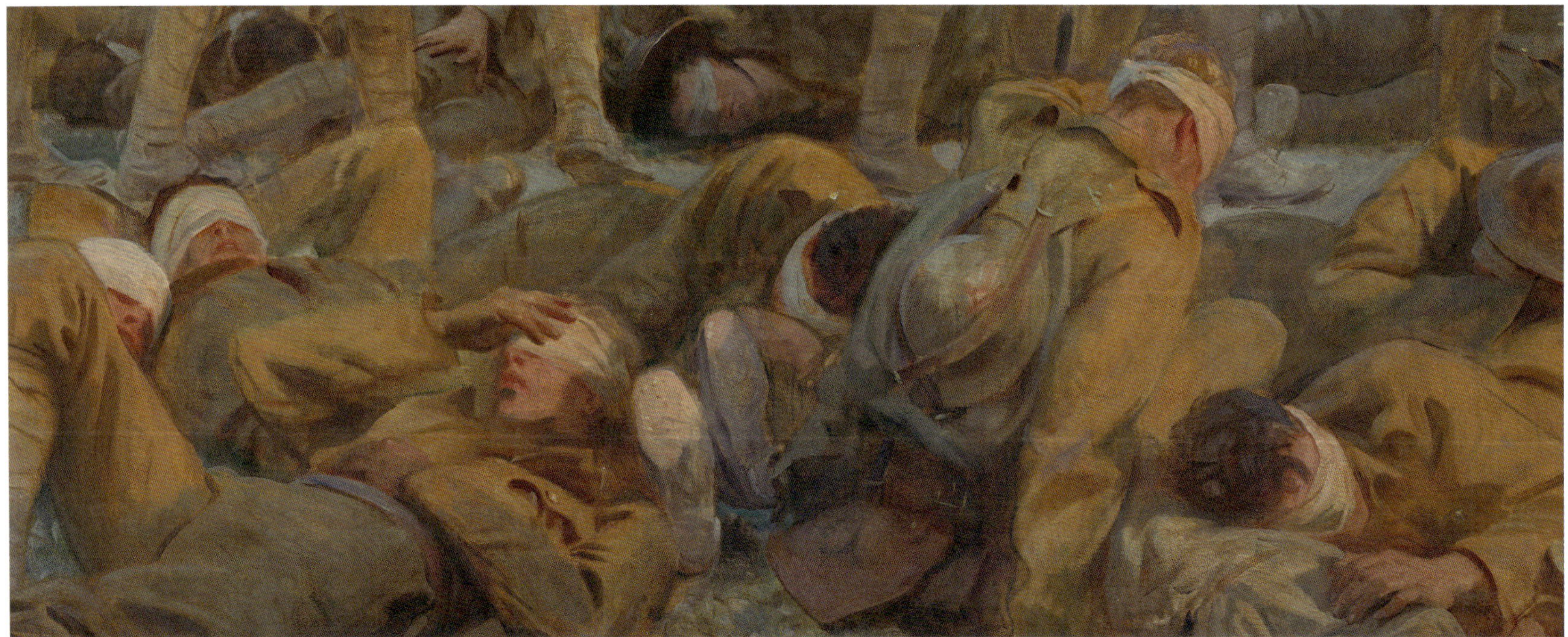

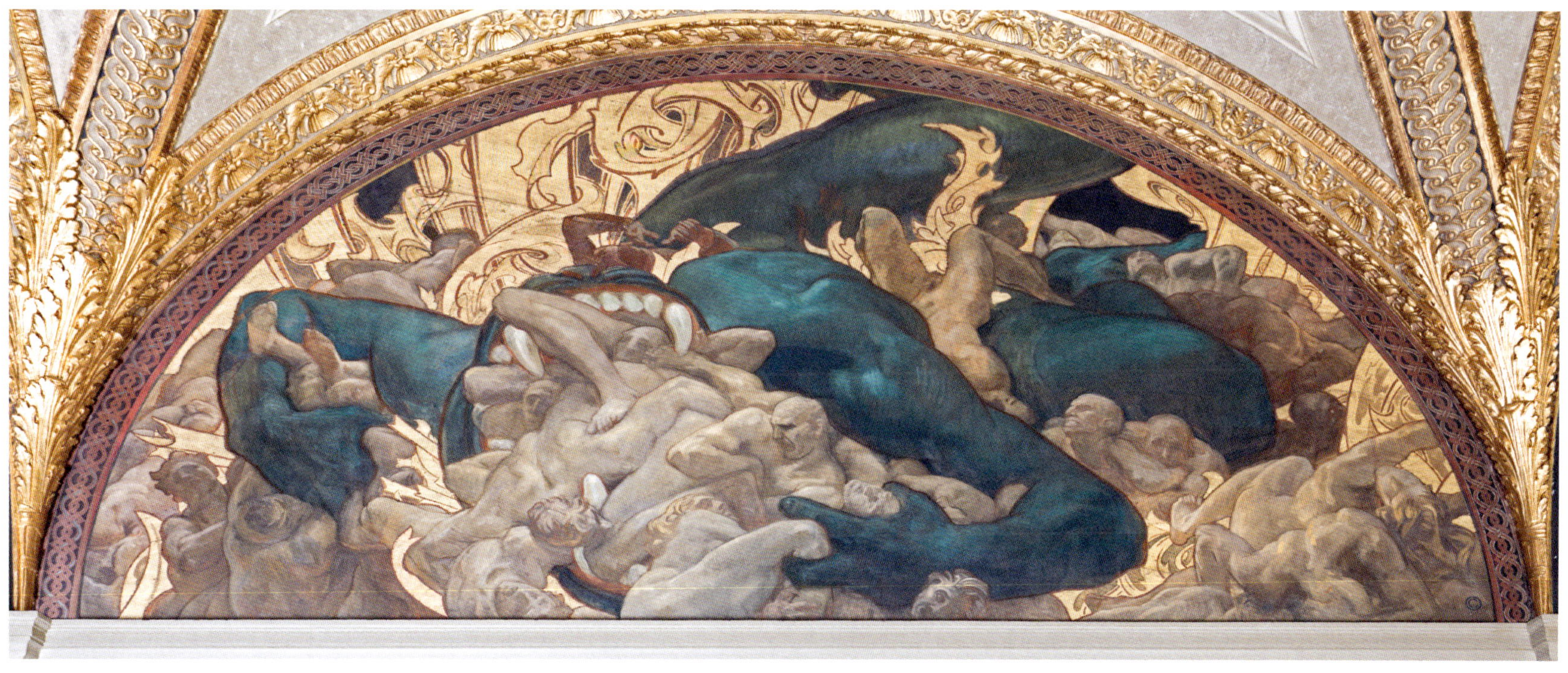

↖↖

Pieter Bruegel the Elder,
***The Parable of the Blind*, 1568 (detail)**

TEMPERA ON LINEN CANVAS
MUSEO DI CAPODIMONTE, NAPLES

Bruegel's audience would have known the biblical story on which this painting is based, as well as other literary references that it contains. Philosopher and theologian Erasmus had published his *Adagia* two years earlier, including a quotation from the Roman poet Horace: '*Caecus caeco dux*' ('the blind leader of the blind'). As with *Gassed*, earthy realism is complemented by classical allusion.

←

Detail of John Singer Sargent, *Gassed* (1919)

OIL ON CANVAS

↖

Luca Signorelli, *The Damned*,
***c.*1499–1502 (detail)**

FRESCO, CHAPEL OF SAN BRIZIO, ORVIETO CATHEDRAL

For this scene Signorelli drew on biblical passages and references from antiquity. The poses and movements of his figures are deliberately exaggerated to echo the classical artists admired during the Renaissance, especially their depictions of the flexed body engaged in battle. Signorelli included erotic and grotesque elements in his fresco, as well as visual puns. Like Sargent, he was celebrated for his striking foreshortening and use of colour; the demon figures are rendered in garish blues, purples and greens.

↑

John Singer Sargent, *Hell Lunette*, 1916, from *Triumph of Religion* mural, 1895–1919

BOSTON PUBLIC LIBRARY

Signorelli's frescos were also a probable reference point in the development of Sargent's mural cycle commission for Boston Public Library, a project that had occupied the artist for the three decades before 1919. In the Library the lunette panel entitled *Hell* bears comparison with Signorelli's fresco and with *Gassed*. In the panel Hell is depicted as a burly green monster, its fangs exposed as it shovels a mass of entwined male bodies into its gaping mouth.

→

John Singer Sargent,
***Crashed Aeroplane,* 1918**

WATERCOLOUR ON PAPER

In the three months after his arrival in France, Sargent completed 35 watercolours of the scenes he saw around him, alongside gathering material for his monumental commission. Here he records a view over fields with a crashed aircraft in the background. In the foreground two labourers gather the crop into bundles; the woman ties the sheaf while the man works with a long-handled scythe. Both are bent over their work, apparently unaffected by the scene behind. Sargent draws a comparison between the aircraft – an emblem of speed and mobility – and the manual, methodical nature of agricultural labour.

This work was among ten that Sargent presented to the IWM in 1919. In a letter to Alfred Yockney on 27 December 1918, he stated: 'I think my watercolours gain from being seen together in a certain quantity, and I would be glad to add to the four you have selected by giving some more. But I would like to have your assurance that they would all be hung, and hung together.'

the concept of an epic – evoking and celebrating myths, legends and histories – with the intermittent action and mundane practical reality of the war's events. It was an experience that seemed, at first, dishearteningly ignoble.

Correspondence in the IWM War Artist Archive reveals that Sargent received a lightning flash of inspiration on 21 August 1918. Fellow artist Henry Tonks, who accompanied him, described how the men witnessed the aftermath of a gas attack and its impact: 'Sargent was very struck by the scene and immediately made a lot of notes'. Sketches and notes were Sargent's working method during his time in France. Before arriving at the subject for *Gassed*, his experiences over three months had already proved fertile ground for making watercolour drawings. Back in London, he continued to work up preparatory studies for *Gassed*. In them he focused on the details of contorted limbs, foreshortened torsos, raised arms, tightly wound puttees and upturned helmets in pursuit of the representation of a mass of men, harmed in their prime, reclining and intermingled in the shared aftermath of battle.

The suggested life-size proportions of the figures caused Sargent trouble. In a letter of October 1918 to Alfred Yockney, Secretary of the BWMC, he lamented the enormity of the task. He noted that 'I think the picture would be infinitely better and much less impossible to execute if it were half the size, and the largest figures half life-size'. Muirhead Bone encouraged Sargent to keep the canvas at a monumental 20 feet long despite the reduction, insisting that 'I feel so keenly that you could give such vividness and sense of life to a large space'.

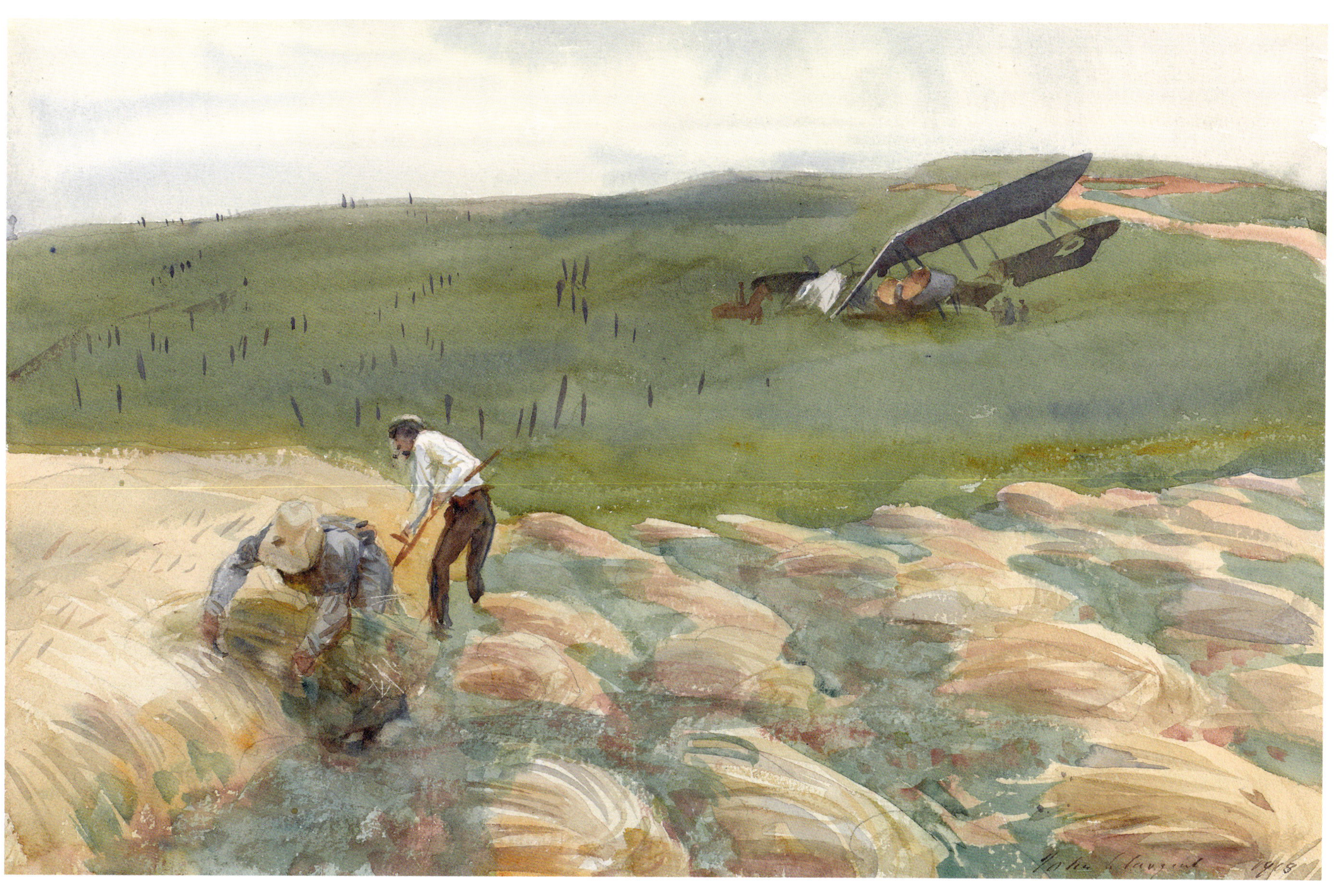

COPY.

Vale Studio B,
Vale Avenue,
Chelsea, S. W. 3.

19th March, 1920.

My dear Yockney,

Sargent and I were staying at Arras at the time. I heard the night before a rumour that the Guards intended to advance the next morning. The exact date in August 1918 I forget but it must have been the latter part. After luncheon we started out in Sargent's car together along the road to Doulens, turning off to make enquiries at the Guards Head Quarters at Bailleumont. We heard that General Fielding had moved his Headquarters to Ransart, we did not go there as we thought he might not want to be disturbed but went towards Blaireville and stopped at a dressing station not very far from there. Sargent made a sketch,but there were very few cases there. After tea we heard that on the Doulens Road at the Corps dressing station at Bac-du-sud there were a good many gassed cases, so we went there. The Dressing Station was situated on the road and consisted of a number of huts and a few tents. Gassed cases kept coming in, lead along in parties of about six just as Sargent has depicted them, by an orderly. They sat or lay down on the grass, there must have been several hundred, evidently suffering

P.T.O.

a great deal, chiefly I fancy from their eyes which were covered up by a piece of lint. The gas was mustard gas which causes temporary blindness from selling of the conjunctiva and lids. Sargent was very struck by the scene and immediately made a lot of notes. It was a very fine evening and the sun toward setting.

↑

Letter from Henry Tonks to Alfred Yockney, 19 March 1920

Tonks described the context for *Gassed* in a letter to Alfred Yockney, Secretary of the BWMC: 'After tea we heard that on the Doullens Road at the Corps dressing at Bac-du-Sud there were a good many gassed cases, so we went there. The dressing station was situated on the road and consisted of a number of huts and a few tents. *Gassed* cases kept coming in, led along in parties of about six just as Sargent has depicted them, by an orderly. They sat or lay down on the grass, there must have been several hundred, evidently suffering a great deal, chiefly I fancy from their eyes which were covered up by a piece of lint ... Sargent was very struck by the scene and immediately made a lot of notes.'

→

A line of infantry blinded by gas, 10 April 1918

These soldiers, of the 55th (West Lancashire) Division, experienced an unusually heavy and prolonged bombardment with gas and explosive shell during the Battle of Estaires. In this photograph they are lined up awaiting treatment at an advanced dressing station near Béthune.

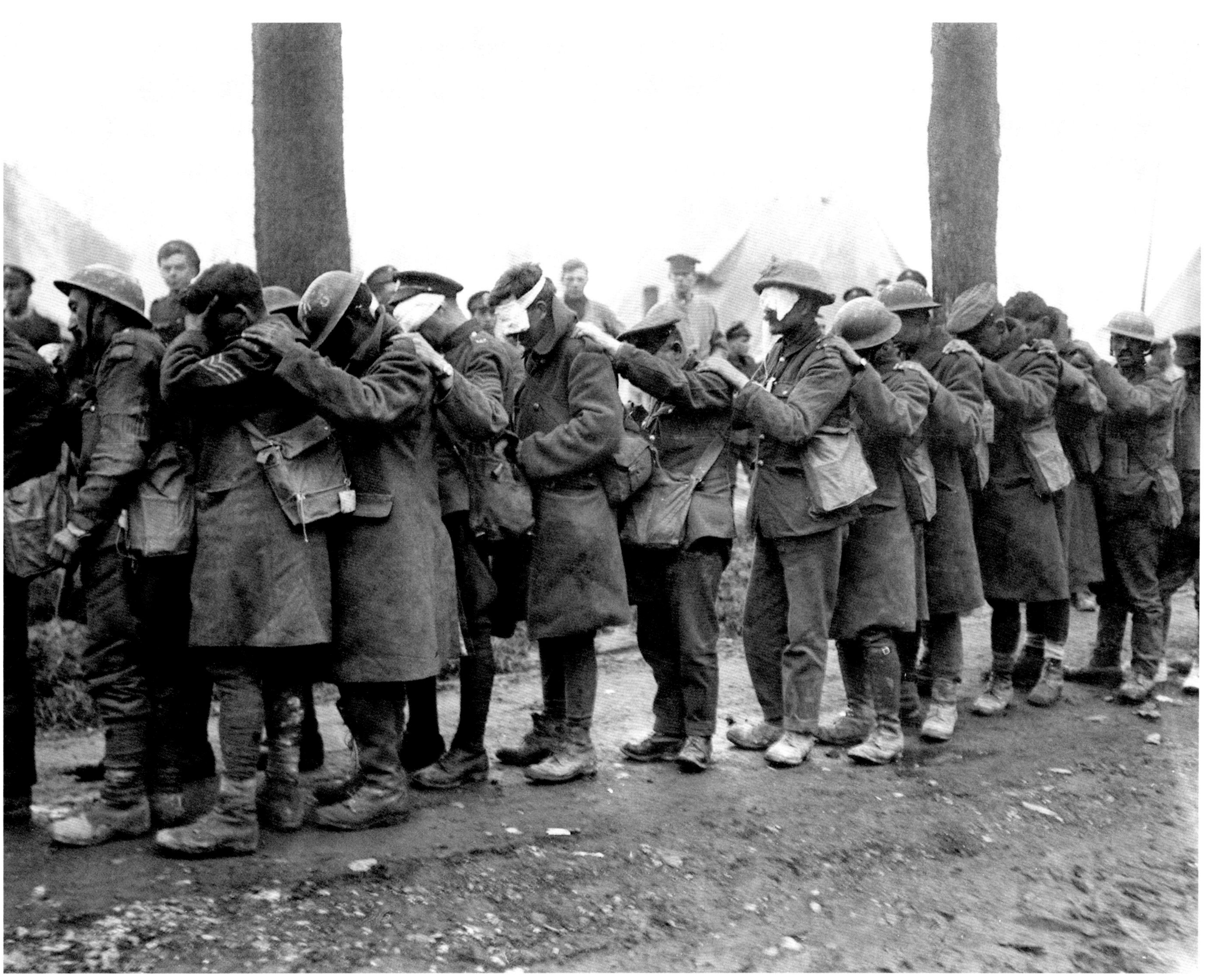

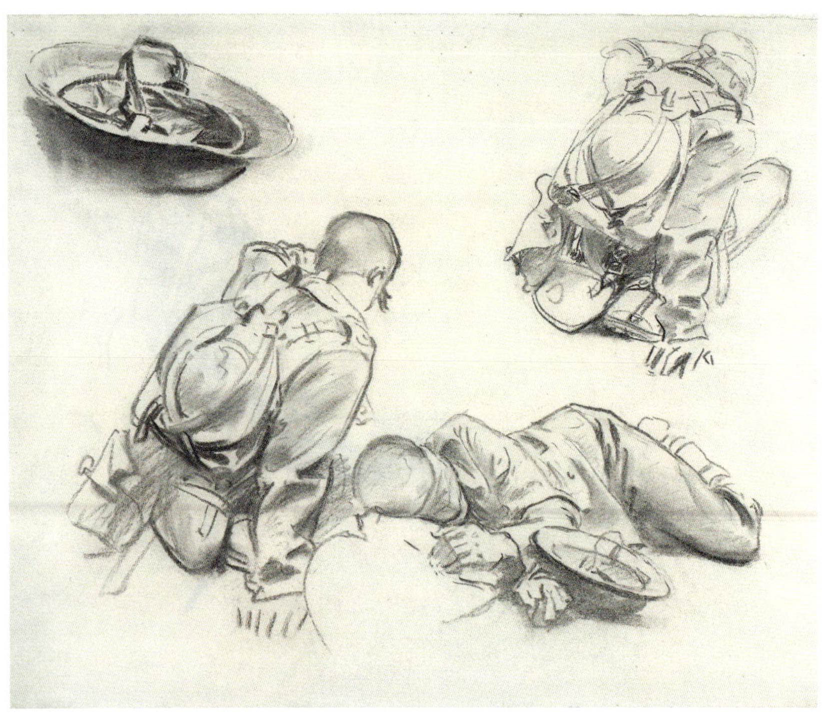

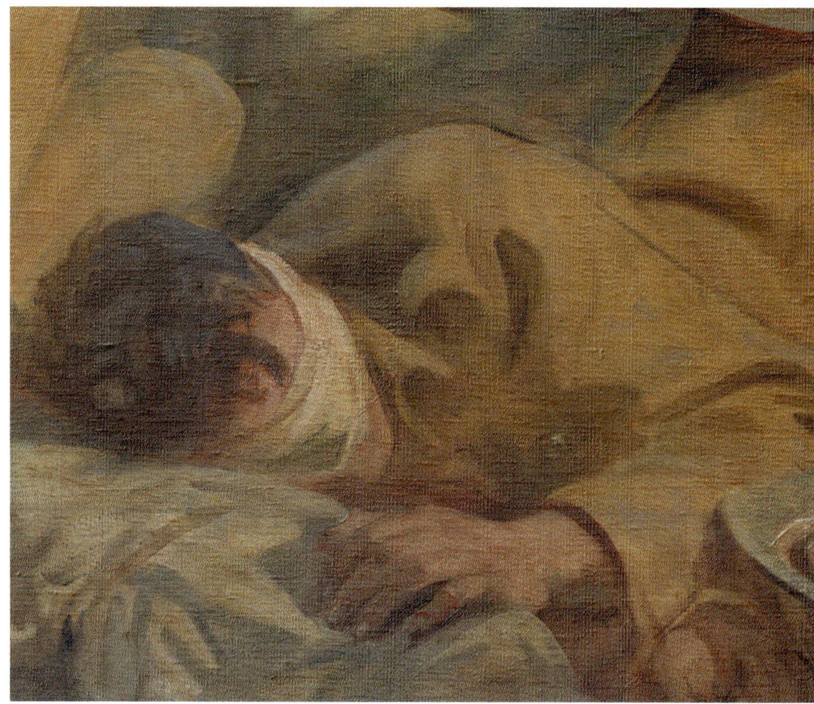

↑
John Singer Sargent, *Study for Gassed: four studies of seated soldiers and a tin hat, c.*1918
CHARCOAL ON PAPER

This quite developed charcoal study includes a detailed study of an upturned tin helmet. Sargent closely observed uniform and kit, as well as the poses of men suffering with the effects of gas warfare. Eyewitness experience for artists was prioritised by the BWMC scheme, as it was thought to enable a more authentic record of war.

In this drawing, the skill of Sargent as a supreme portrait painter is evident. He pays close attention to the heads and torsos of the seated and reclining figures, imbuing them with a sense of forbearance and dignity. He recalls Renaissance precedents in the use of *contrapposto* (or 'counterpoise', as the shoulder twists off-axis), drawing together the real-life suffering he witnessed on the Western Front with the poetic ideals of classical beauty.

↑
Detail of John Singer Sargent, *Gassed,* 1919
OIL ON CANVAS

→
John Singer Sargent, *Study for Gassed: soldier and kit, c.*1918
CHARCOAL ON PAPER

This study describes the head and upper body of a British soldier suffering from the effects of gas and lying on his side on the ground. His head rests on a pile of his kit; his eyes are covered by a bandage. Above this is a lighter sketch of various equipment, including a water bottle and upturned steel helmet. The study relates to a figure shown sleeping on his hands in the painting.

Though Sargent was committed to authentic representation of the suffering he had witnessed following a gas attack in August 1918, the figures in both his preparatory studies and the final painting are stoic and calm.

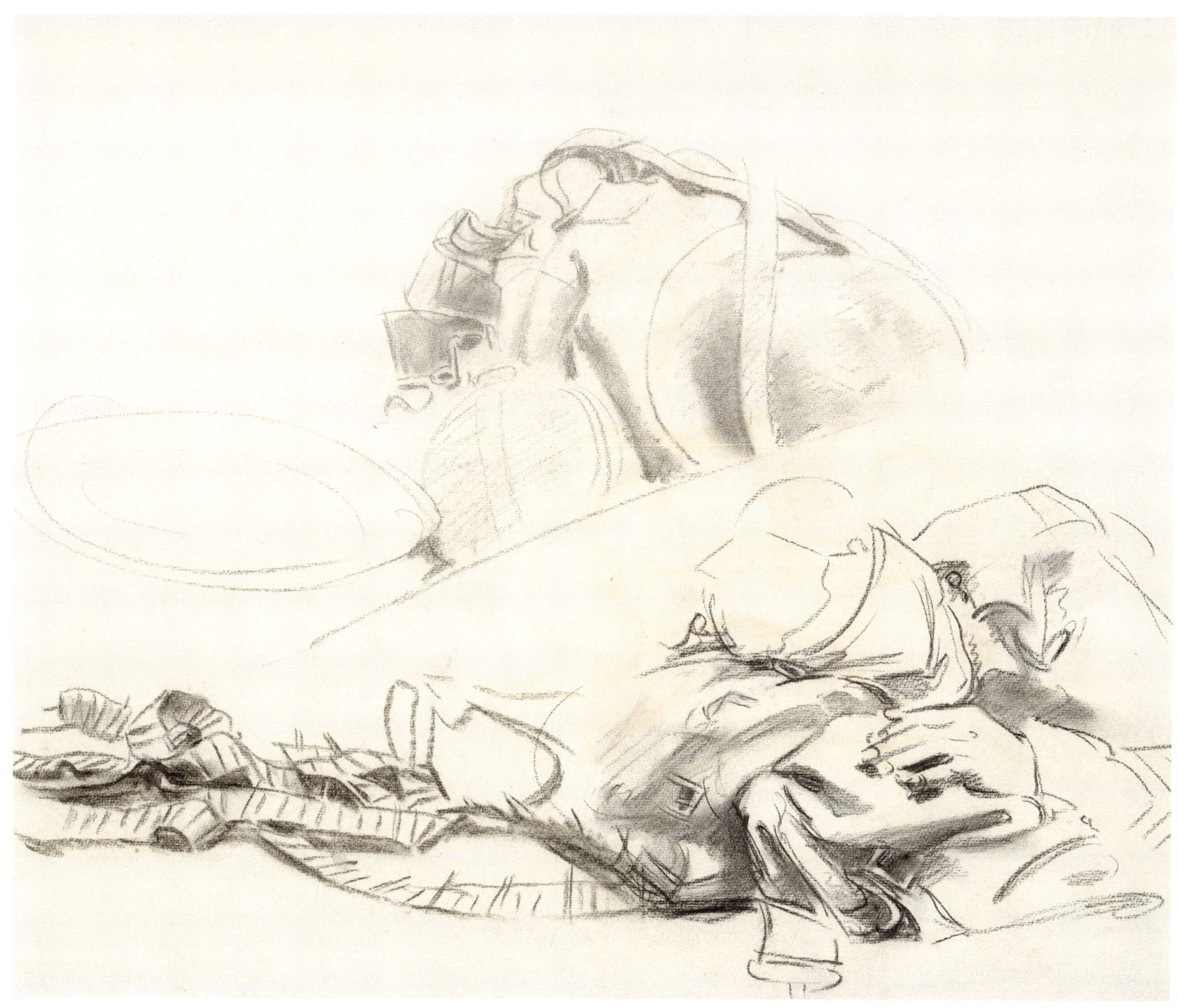

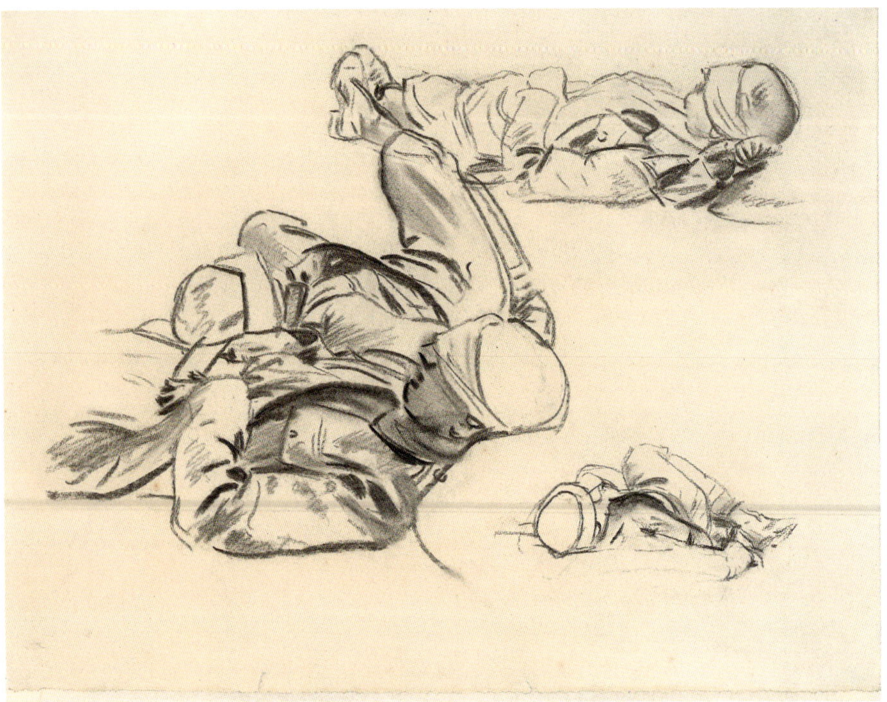

←

John Singer Sargent, *Study for Gassed: three studies of soldiers with bandaged heads*, c.1918

CHARCOAL ON PAPER

This charcoal sketch is made up of three studies of British soldiers suffering from the effects of exposure to gas and lying on the ground. The soldiers lie with their heads resting on improvised pillows made of blankets and equipment, their eyes covered with bandages.

In his preparatory studies Sargent worked out the relationships between men in his painting. This was important for the structure and balance of the overall composition, and for Sargent's ambition to create a modern epic representative of the profound experience of war. He thought this was best achieved by using motifs found in art history and creating a work that included 'masses of men'.

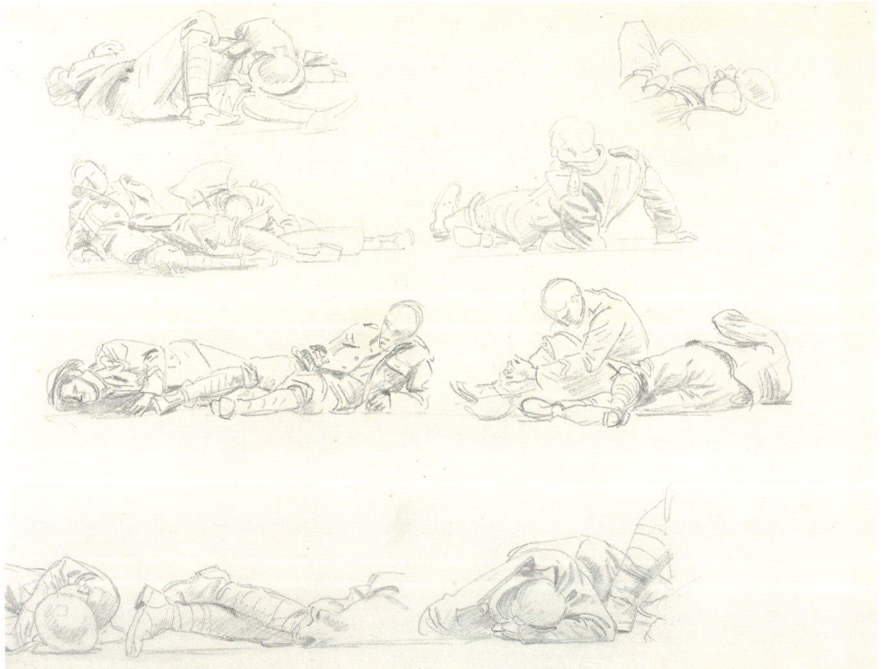

←

John Singer Sargent, *Study for Gassed: eight studies of soldiers*, c.1918

PENCIL ON PAPER

This pencil drawing comprises eight studies of reclining or lying figures. One soldier rests his head on his folded arm; another is propped up on his elbow. Sargent's careful observations here informed the group of interlinked bodies suffering from exposure to gas in the foreground of the painting. The artist transposed the figure at far left, his face turned out to the viewer, into the centre of the painting and covered his eyes with a bandage.

The figures in this study have a timeless quality. It has been observed that – as in the painting – the figures do not seem to belong to a particular group in the contemporary world, even though the inclusion of uniform and kit roots them in the time and space of the First World War. Instead, Sargent shapes the mass of lying and reclining bodies into a frieze, recalling classical forms and imagery.

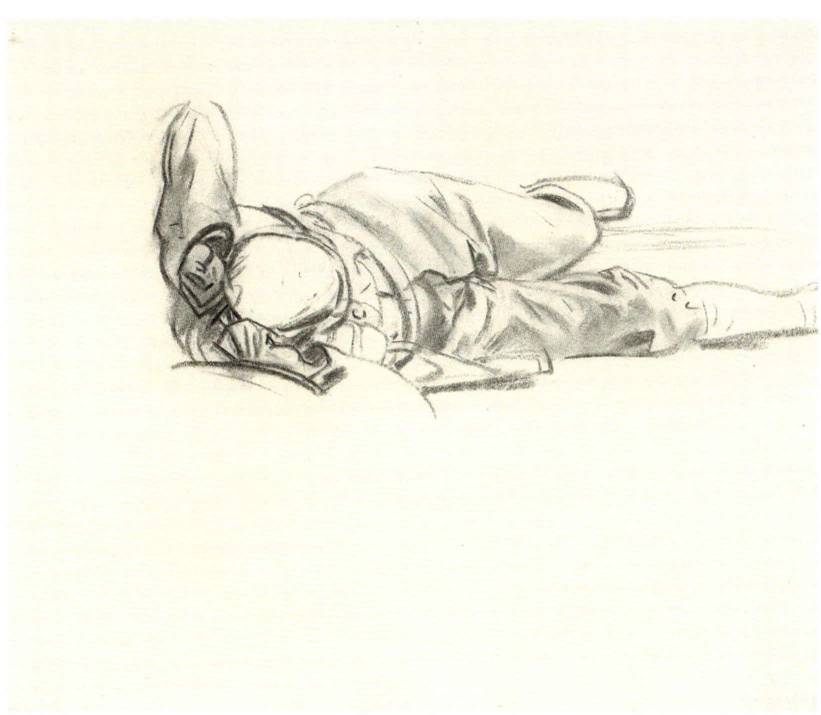

↑

John Singer Sargent, *Study for Gassed: reclining soldier with bandaged head, c.*1918

CHARCOAL ON PAPER

This study of a British soldier, lying on the ground on his side with an elbow raised and facing skyward, is the basis for a soldier represented at the lower right foreground of *Gassed*. His head is supported with an improvised pillow made of his pack and his eyes appear to be bandaged.

This graceful figure, though lying down, takes a *contrapposto* form, a term that usually refers to a standing figure carrying weight on one leg, causing the other hip to rise and the knee to bend, and a rotation on the axis of the body. In ancient Greek visual culture, the relationship between the tense and relaxed limbs expressed a deeper significance about humanity and psychological disposition. It demonstrates Sargent's commitment to art historical citation.

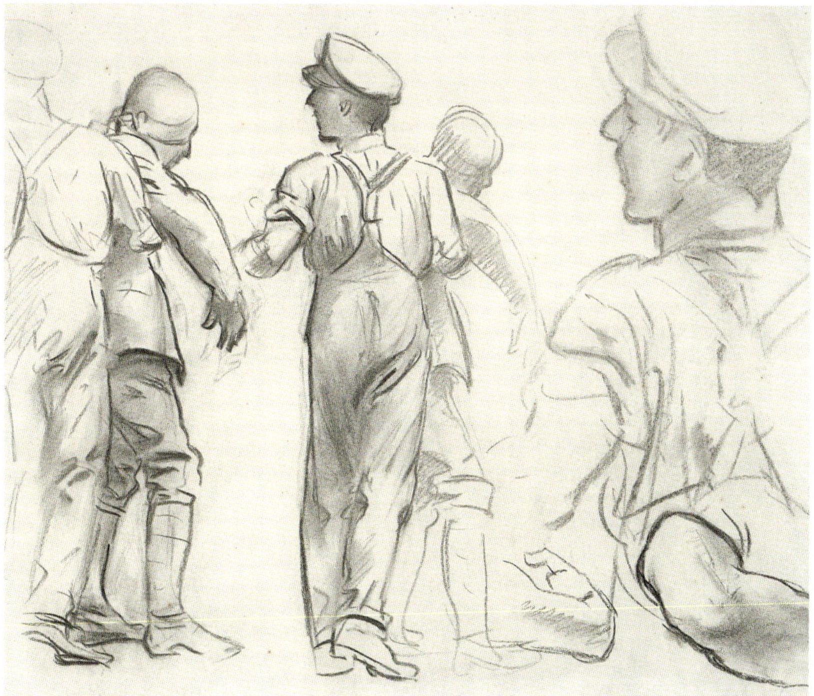

↑

John Singer Sargent, *Study for Gassed: studies of a medical orderly and wounded men, c.*1918

CHARCOAL ON PAPER

These studies depict a medical orderly holding and supporting a gassed British soldier under the right armpit. Included here are two almost identical depictions of the two men, with a detailed study of the orderly in close-up to the right and a detail of his elbow in the bottom right.

Though he is rooted in the First World War in terms of clothing, the figure in this study twists left, with his right leg raised, recalling the *contrapposto* pose of Renaissance sculpture and images from antiquity. He is more upright than the other figures, neatly dressed and in control, appropriate to his redemptive role in *Gassed* as a medic.

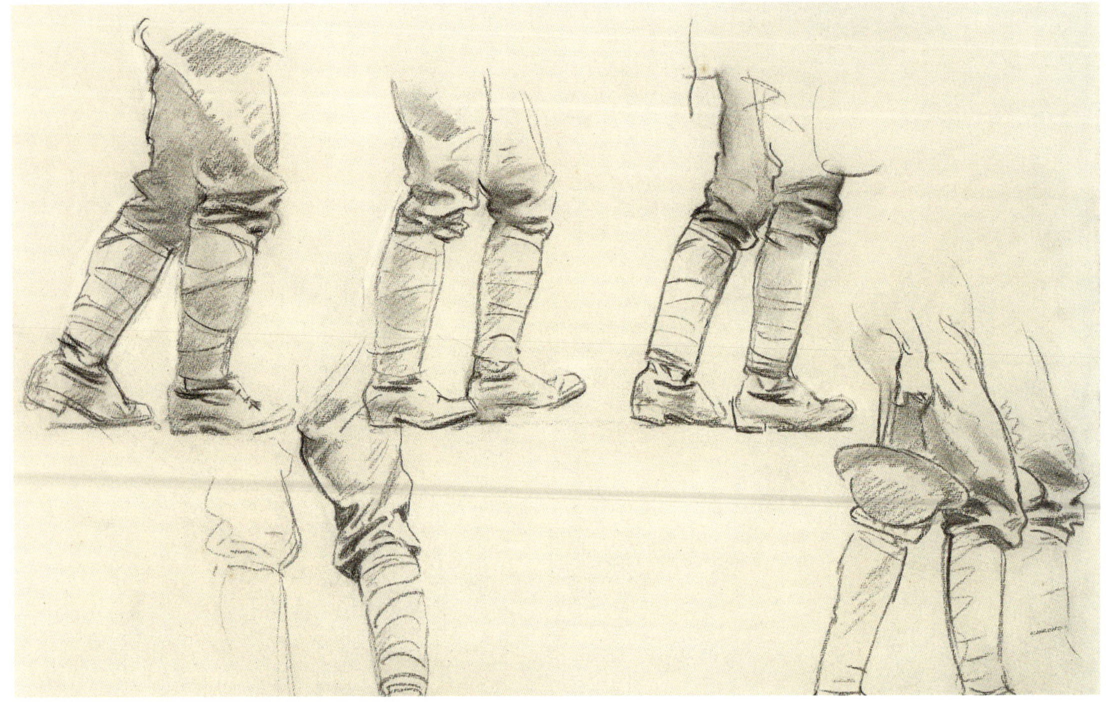

←

John Singer Sargent, *Study for Gassed: five studies of legs, c.*1918

CHARCOAL ON PAPER

The five studies of legs mainly appear to be studies of the same British soldier. He is wearing puttees – coverings of the lower part of the leg made from a long, narrow piece of cloth wound tightly around the leg – and boots. The five preparatory studies each focus on a different moment of motion. They inform the central, frieze-like section of the oil painting, which portrays the slow and cumbersome movement of gas victims from left to right.

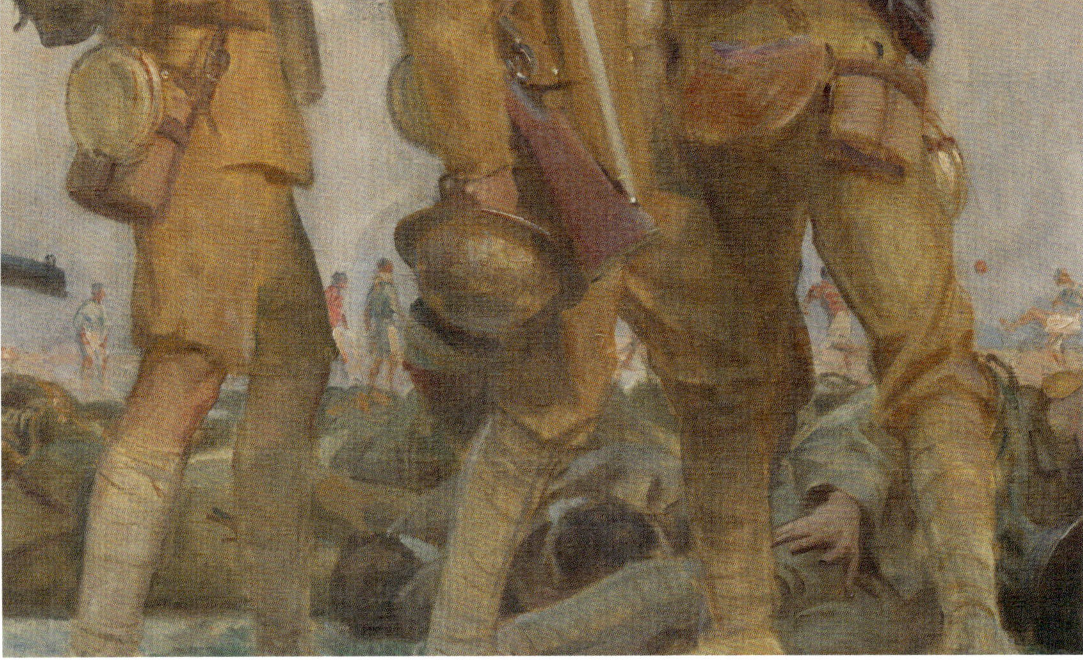

←

Detail of John Singer Sargent, *Gassed,* 1919

OIL ON CANVAS

→

John Singer Sargent, *Study for Gassed: three studies of a soldier drinking from his water bottle, c.*1918

CHARCOAL ON PAPER

For these three studies of a British soldier drinking from a water bottle, Sargent used the same soldier. The drawings focus wholly on the head, with the man's right hand holding the water bottle to his lips. Here Sargent paid close attention to the effect of foreshortening on the hand, face and bottle. The combined elements appear in the crowd of bodies in the foreground of the painting.

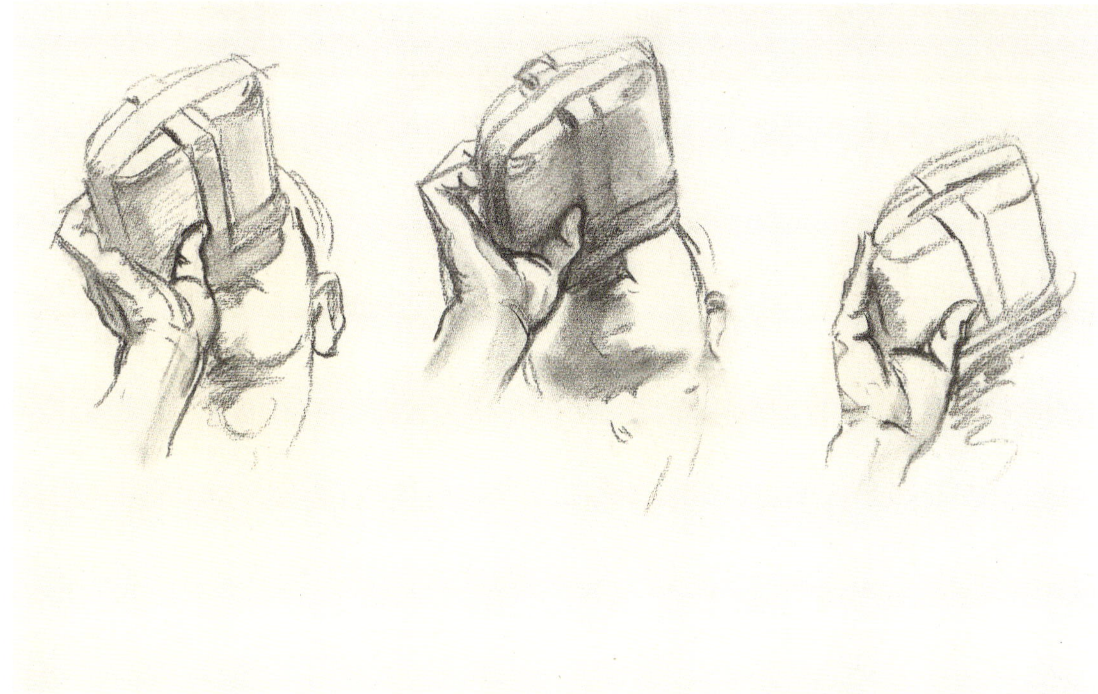

→

Detail of John Singer Sargent, *Gassed,* 1919

OIL ON CANVAS

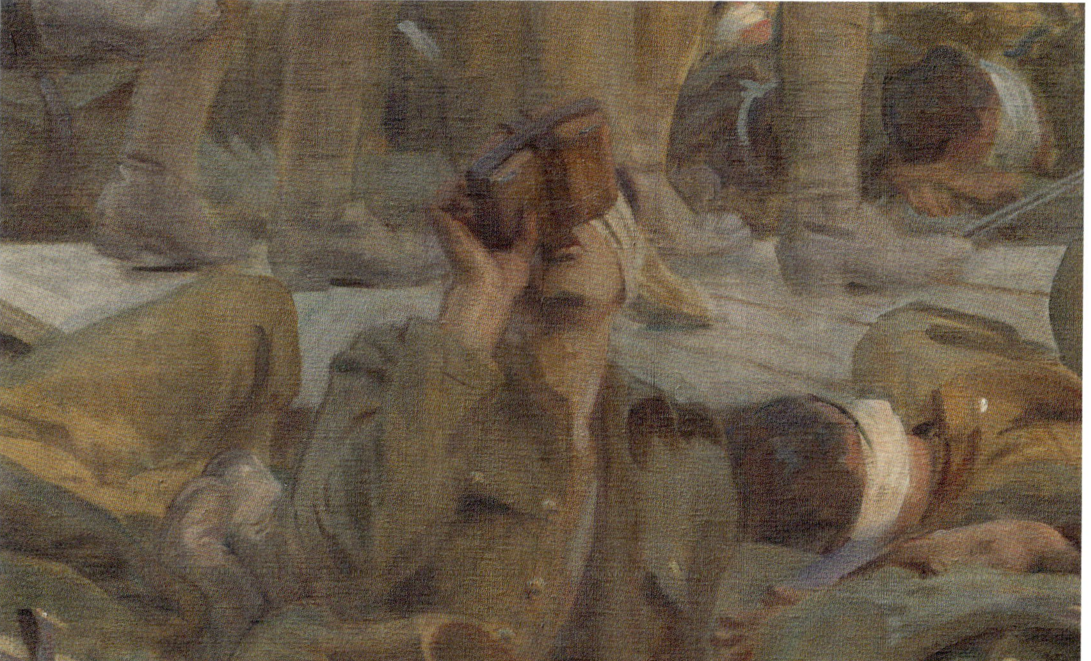

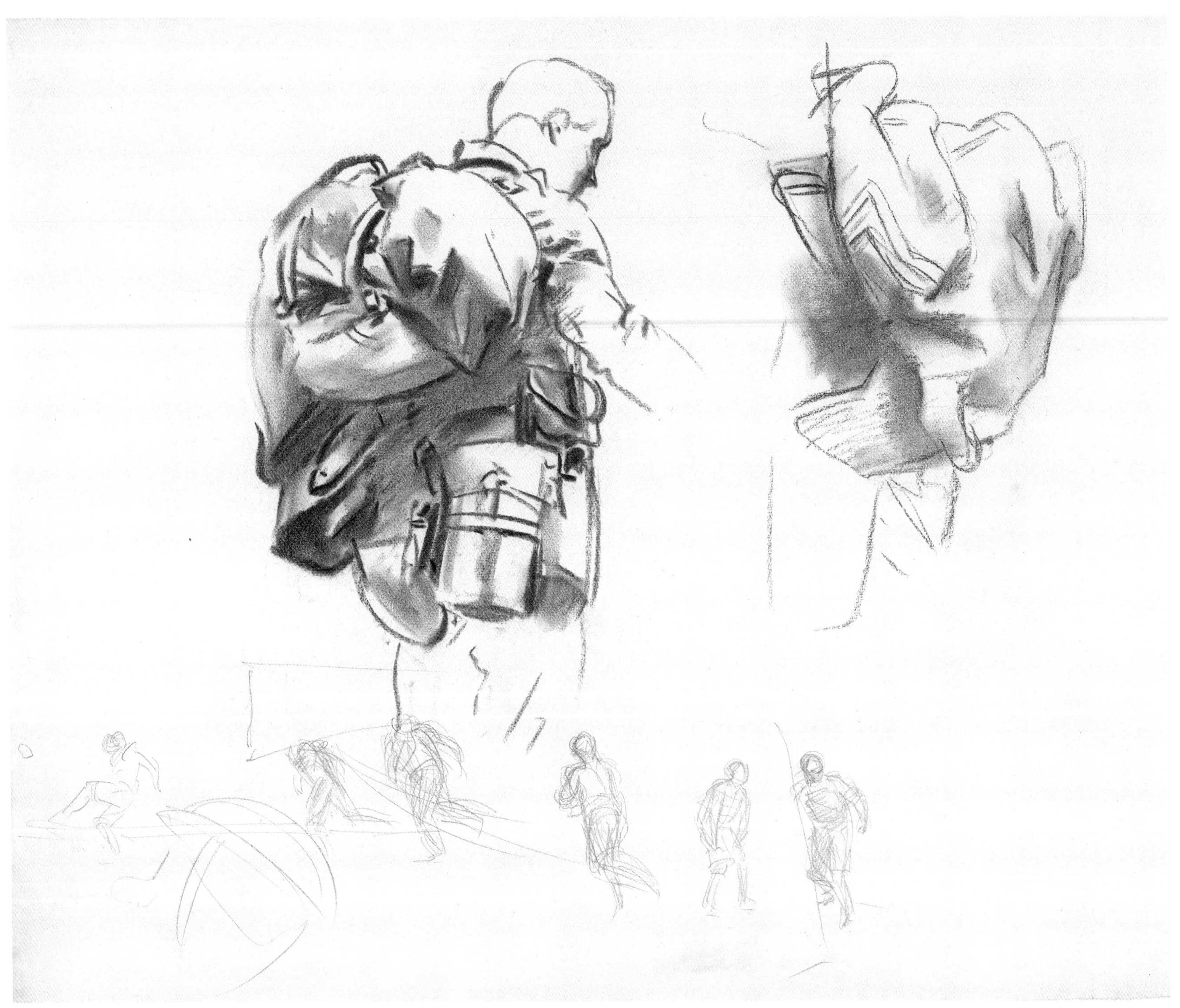

←

John Singer Sargent, *Study for Gassed*: *half-length study of soldier in full kit plus drawings of soldiers playing football, c.*1918

PENCIL AND CHARCOAL ON PAPER

This detailed study describes an infantryman seen from behind and fully laden with equipment. The inclusion of a British infantryman's tunic suggests Sargent's close observation during his time in France. A loose pencil sketch of a football match in progress informs the background scene of *Gassed*.

The figure relates to a soldier near the front of the line being led along the duckboard, gripped by an upright orderly with his back to the viewer. In the painted context, the figure has a covering over his eyes and the addition of a tin helmet.

↓ →

Details of John Singer Sargent, *Gassed*, 1919

OIL ON CANVAS

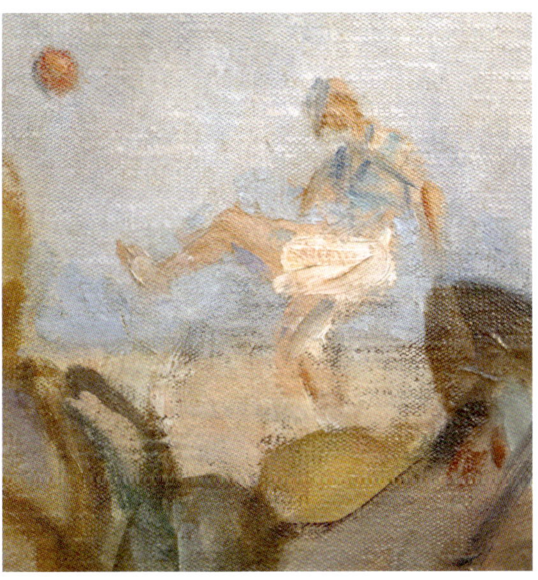

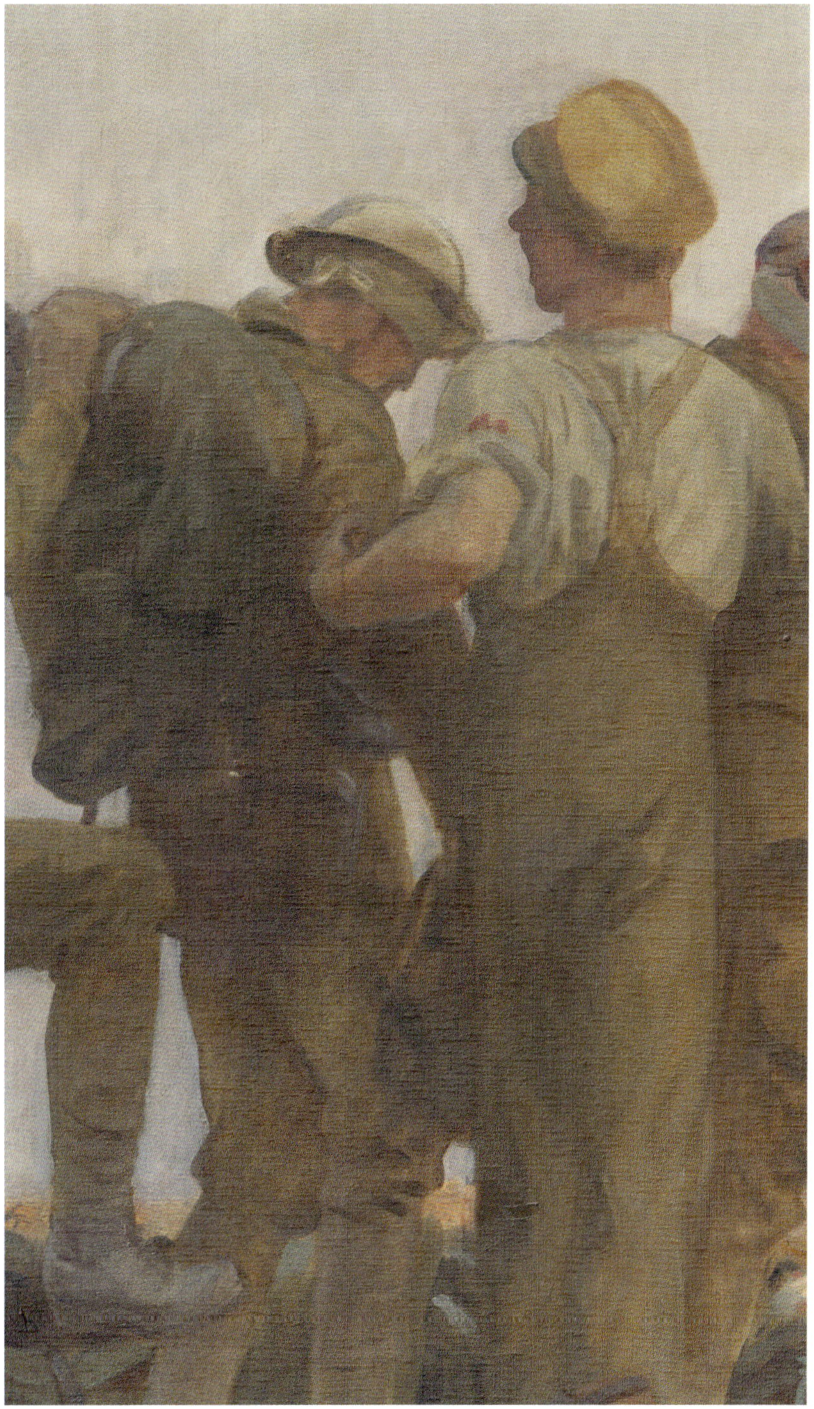

→

Anna Airy, *A Shell Forge at a National Projectile Factory, Hackney Marshes, London*, 1918

OIL ON CANVAS

This painting was exhibited in the 1918 Summer Exhibition at the Royal Academy which also included *Gassed*. It depicts the interior of a shell forge and shows the hot shell cases emerging from furnaces at the left of the composition. The work was a particular challenge for artist Anna Airy, one of the few officially commissioned female war artists in the First World War. She preferred to work from life and had to work at great speed to capture the colour and form of molten metal. The extreme heat of the factory added to the intensity. Describing her experience, Airy said, 'I've never felt such heat! The floor got "black-hot". I burnt a pair of shoes right off my feet!'

In June 1918 Airy was commissioned by the Munitions Committee at the newly founded IWM to create four paintings representing typical scenes in four factories, including at Hackney Marshes. She was offered £250 per painting, significantly less than her male counterparts who usually received £300 per painting. Sargent received £600 for *Gassed* due to its monumental size.

[CONTINUED FROM PAGE 46]

Gassed's solemnity and largeness has informed its display in the decades since its production. It was seen first at the Royal Academy in its Summer Exhibition of 1919, then appeared later that year in an exhibition of 'War Pictures'. This included diverse works by many of the artists now found in the IWM collection, among them Anna Airy and George Clausen, Thomas C. Dugdale, Charles Sims and John Lavery. *Gassed* was the subject of much interest; it was nominated for, and subsequently won, Picture of the Year. The Summer Exhibition incited discussion about the place of art in the service of the nation and its role in a post-war world, concepts about which the emerging avant-garde was more dubious. Virginia Woolf, reviewing the exhibition in *The Athenaeum*, criticised its emotional toll, which reached a peak in front of *Gassed*:

> in order to emphasize his point that soldiers wearing bandages round their eyes cannot see, and therefore claim our compassion, he makes one of them raise his leg to the level of his elbow in order to mount a step an inch or two above the ground. This little piece of over-emphasis was the final scratch of the surgeon's knife ... From first to last each canvas had rubbed in some emotion, and what the paint failed to say the catalogue had enforced in words.[22]

By 1920, when the IWM opened its first more permanent premises at Crystal Palace, Sargent's canvas had become a firm favourite with audiences – and it received pride of place. Many former soldiers who had encountered gas themselves felt it did justice to the real experience, and at the same time did something to elevate their story and suffering; the painting certainly has a strong connection to the documentary photography produced at the time. *Gassed* has continued to provoke questions and draw admiration for more than a hundred years. Though the Hall of Remembrance was never built, within the IWM collection the painting has provided a focus for storytelling about the First World War. Overlaying an authentic, eyewitness record with a powerful classical narrative, *Gassed* served to romanticise a very unromantic war and bathe it in early evening sunlight. It also

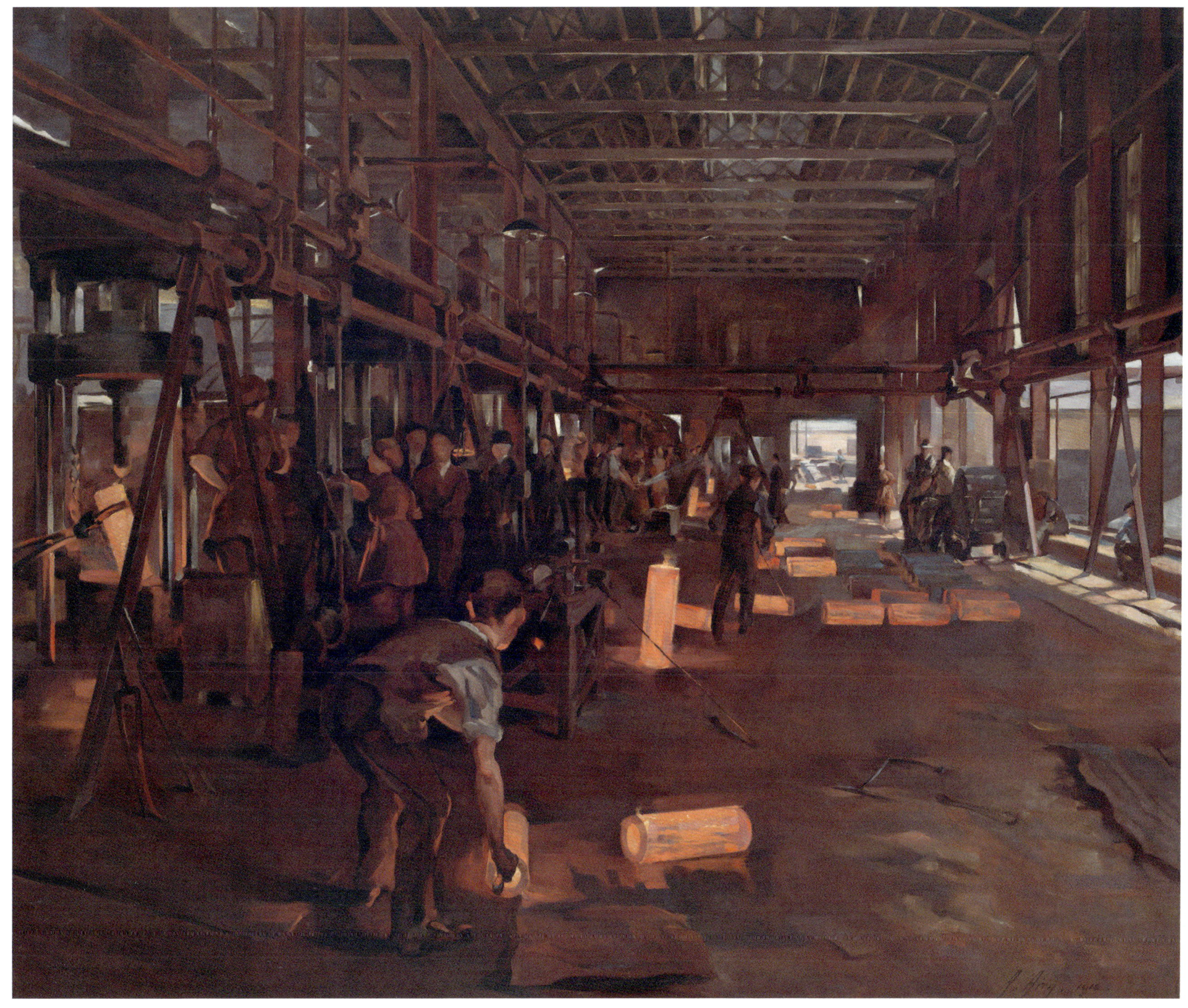

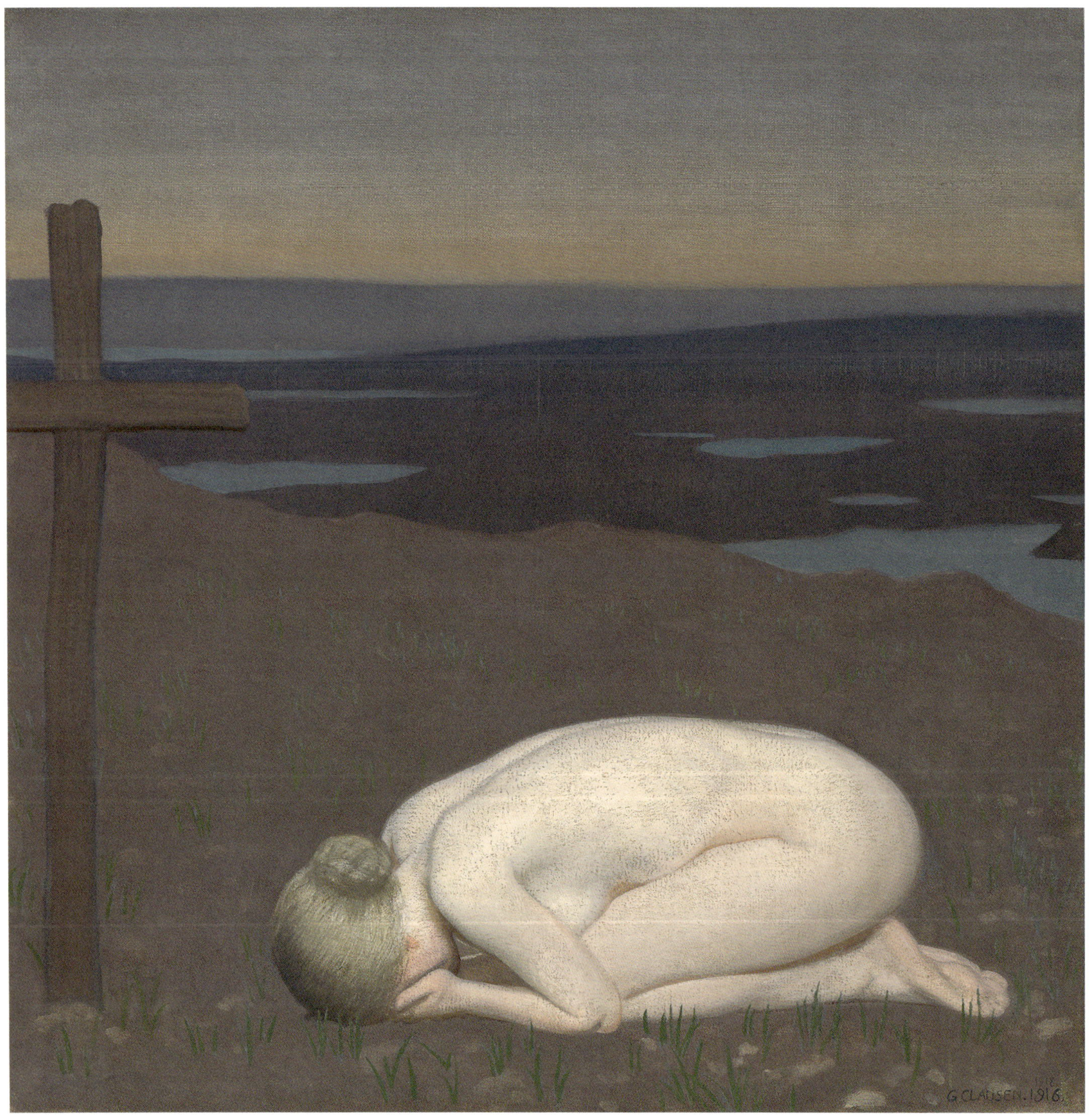
G.CLAUSEN.1916.

←

George Clausen, *Youth Mourning*, 1916

OIL ON CANVAS

In this painting a naked female figure personifies Youth. She kneels before a wooden cross marking a grave. Filled battlefield craters in the background root the work in the First World War. *Youth Mourning* represents a return to a pastoral naturalism – scenes of rustic life as well as rural poverty – for which Clausen had been known early in his career. The painting is a response to the horrors of war, and in particular to the death of his daughter Kitty's fiancé, killed in action at Neuve Chapelle in March 1915, shortly after arrival at the front. Clausen used the central figure's nakedness to emphasise the grief and emptiness of the personal – but also national – experience of loss.

Clausen was commissioned by the BWMC to work on scenes of British industry on the home front. A monumental work, *In the Gun Factory at Woolwich Arsenal*, 1918, is the single outcome and commemorated Britain's largest munitions factory. *Youth Mourning* is a far more personal reflection on war and was not part of the scheme. Exhibited alongside *Gassed* in the 1919 Royal Academy Summer Exhibition, the work was eventually gifted to IWM in 1929.

↗

***Gassed* on display at the Imperial War Museum, Crystal Palace, *c.*1921**

By 1924 four million people had visited the Imperial War Museum's galleries at Crystal Palace, shown here. However, the Palace's glass structure provided too unstable an environment for collections in the longer term; the museum clearly needed to find a new location and downsize radically. The Western Galleries at the Imperial Institute in South Kensington were offered as a new venue – with BWMC oil paintings, including *Gassed*, a priority for display.

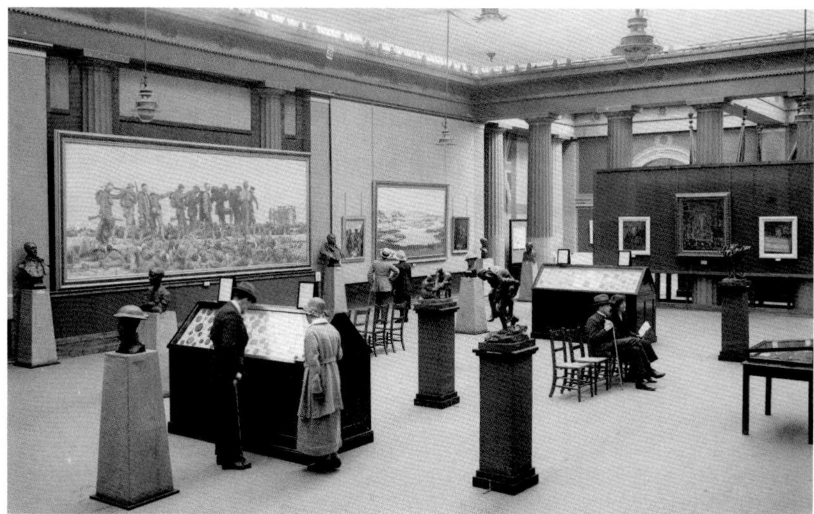

gave purpose to history painting: to act as an immersive site for reflection on personal feelings of loss and sacrifice in the following years; and then, more recently, as a catalyst for understanding about the First World War.

In recent decades *Gassed* was displayed in what became known as 'the Sargent room' at IWM London. In the 2010s this included a dialogue between Sargent's work and Steve McQueen's *Queen and Country*, completed in 2007 following his war artist commission four years previously. McQueen's work comprises a wooden stamp cabinet containing replica sheets of stamps; all feature portrait photograph images of British military personnel who died on active service in the Iraq War. Conceived a century after *Gassed*, McQueen's work also meditates on the themes of loss and remembrance, questioning ideas of sacrifice and nationhood. In 2014–2015 the exhibition *Truth and Memory*, held in the same space, explored a range of British artistic contributions from the First World War before *Gassed* was deinstalled from IWM London for an international tour of North America in 2016.

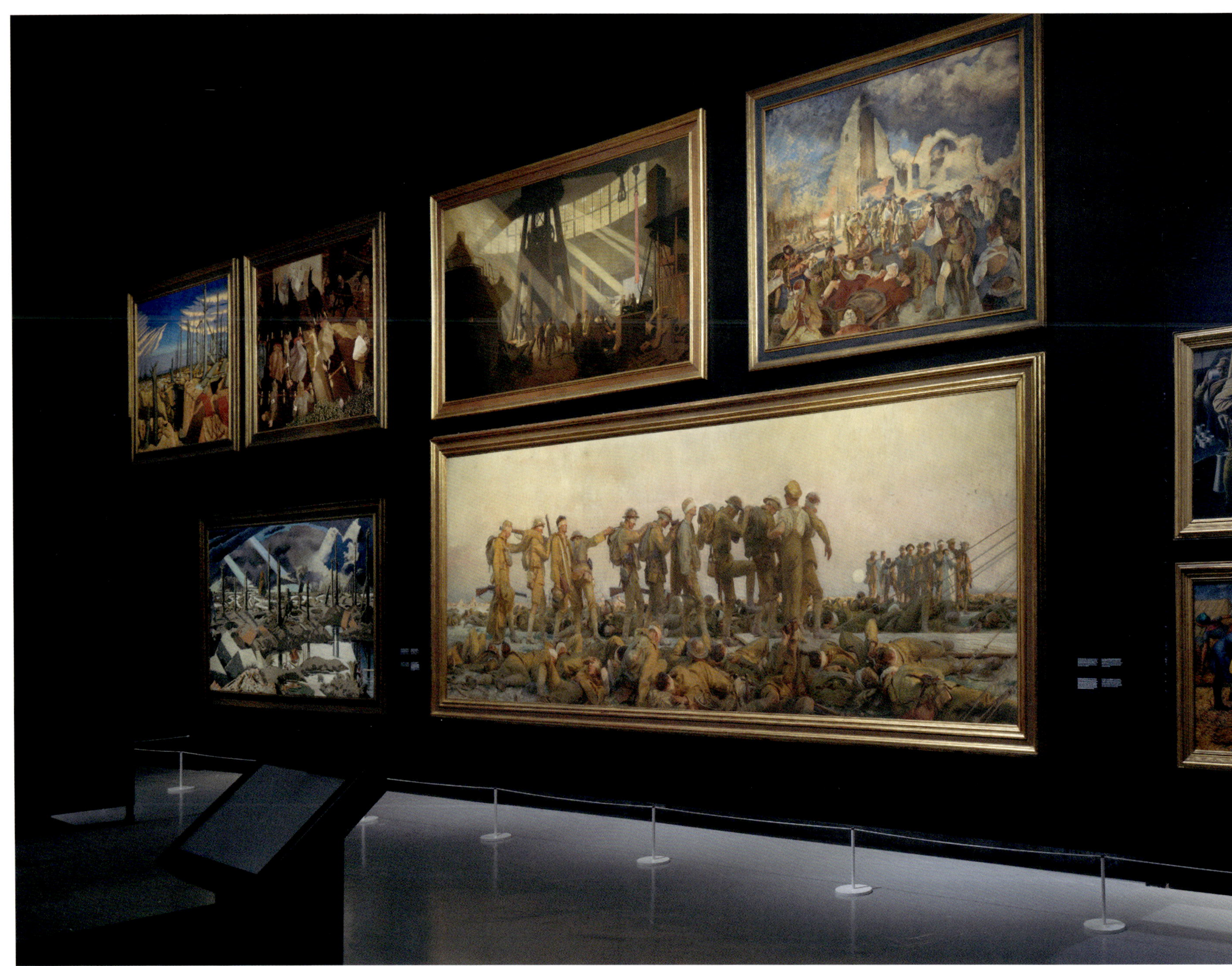

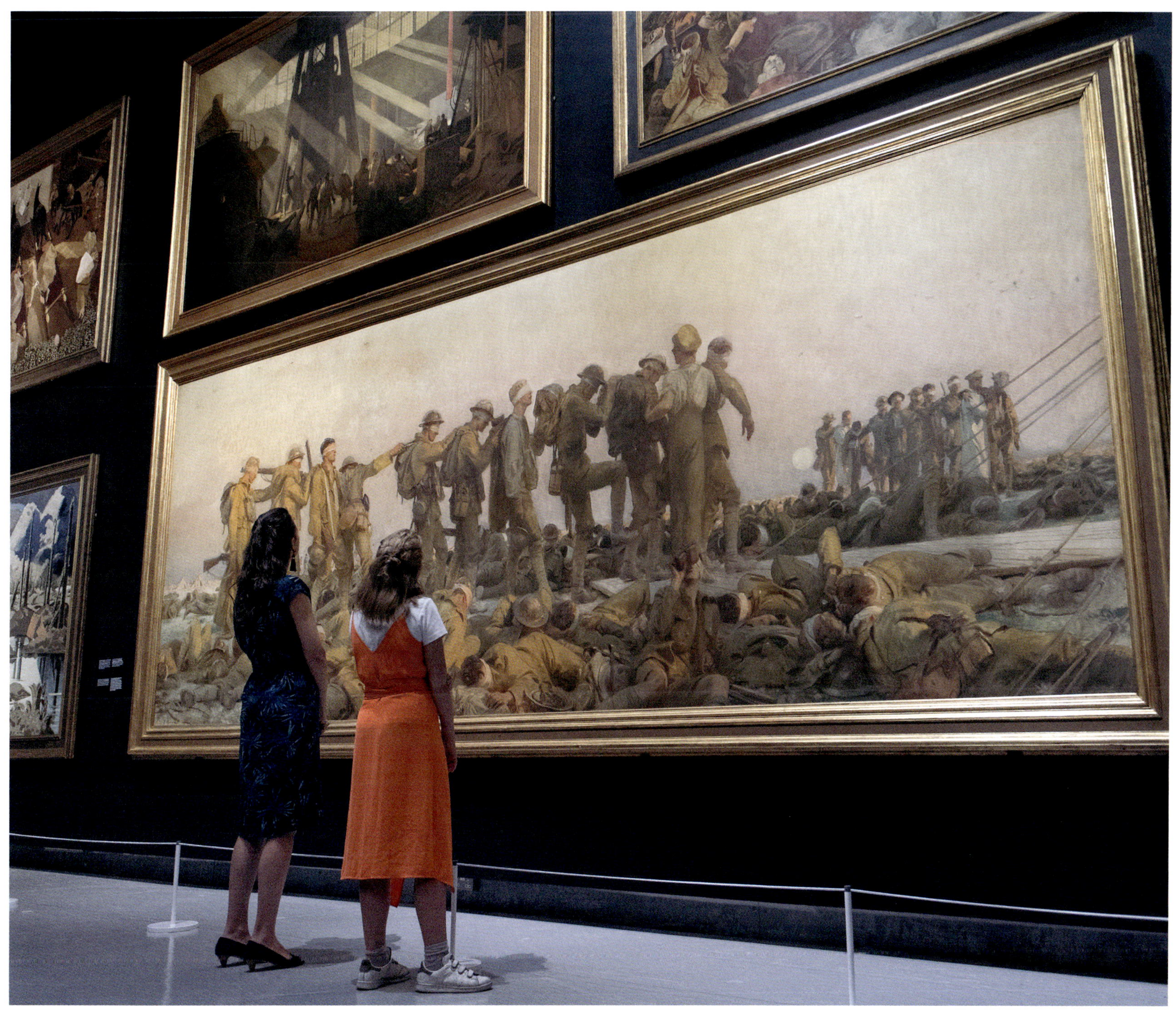

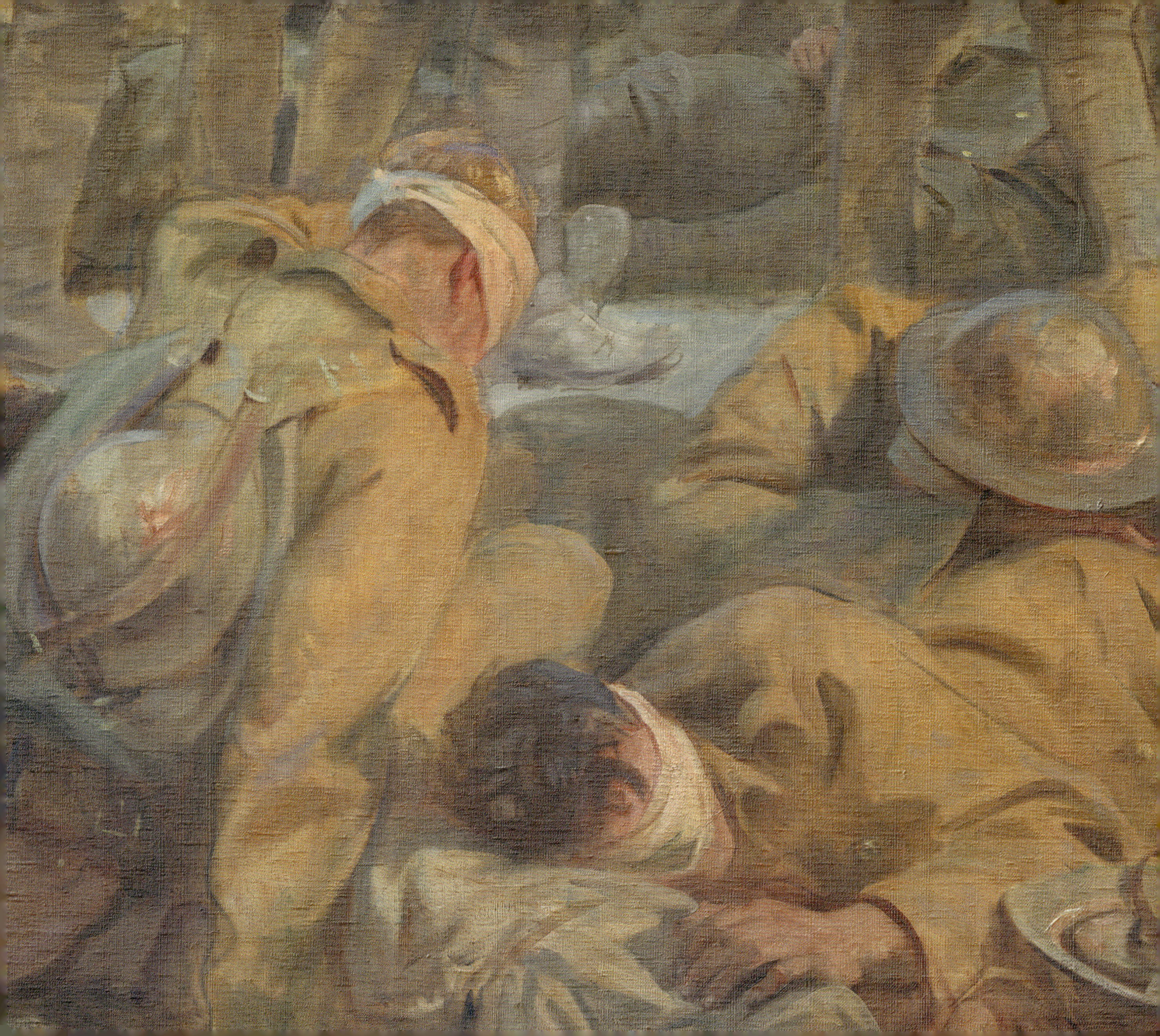

PRESERVING FOR THE FUTURE

Significant conservation and cutting-edge imaging undertaken during 2022 and 2023 has revitalised and transformed the viewing experience of *Gassed*. The processes have simultaneously taken us closer to the experience of its first audiences in 1919 and revealed, as never before, minuscule details of Sargent's materials, surface and process.

Explored further and illustrated in the following pages, expert analysis of both painting and frame has provided new information about Sargent's narrative intent and meticulous construction of *Gassed*. The removal of 40-year-old discoloured varnish and unoriginal, over-bright gilding from the frame has exposed subtleties that have not been witnessed by recent audiences.

Gassed is now on show in a brand new space at IWM London. The Blavatnik Art, Film and Photography Galleries focus on the experiences of visual practitioners of all kinds working in the context of war. Freshly conserved, *Gassed* remains a centrepiece for the IWM displays in these new spaces and holds up as a relevant, incisive account of human conflict.

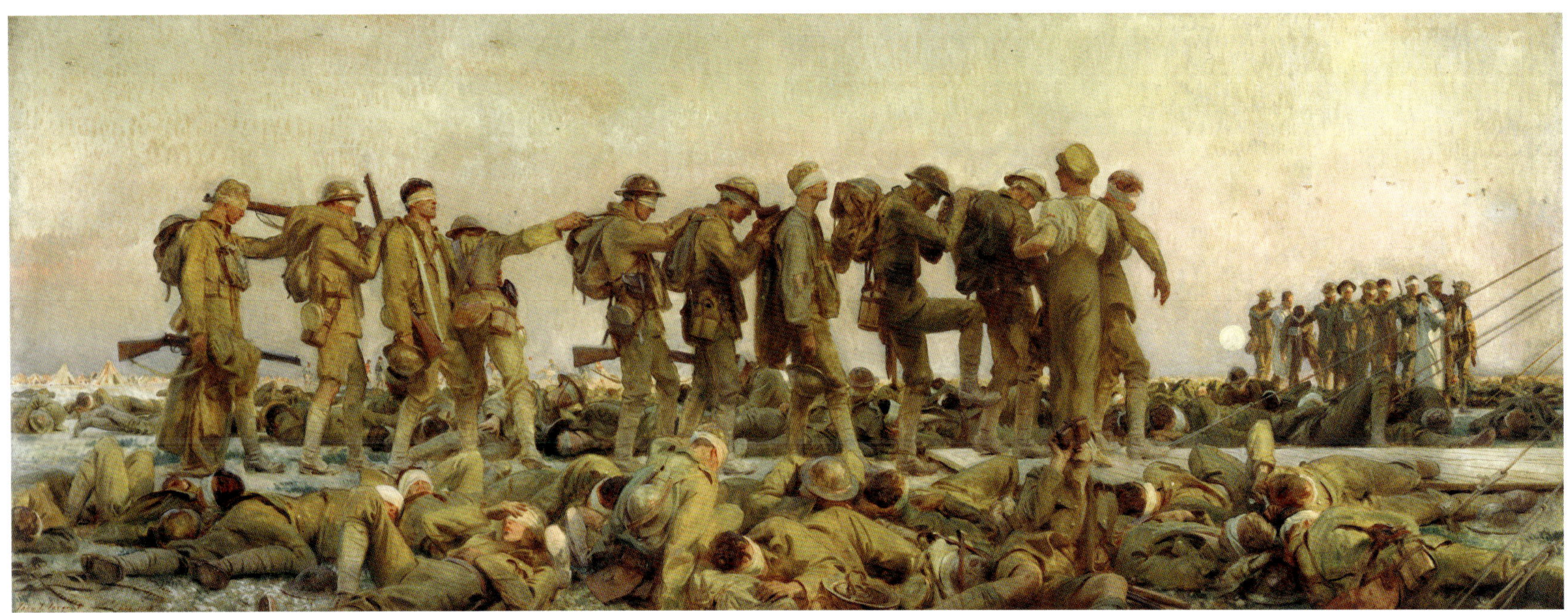

↑
John Singer Sargent, *Gassed*, 1919
OIL ON CANVAS
This image was taken before the conservation work that took place on *Gassed* in 2022 and 2023. Varnish applied in the 1970s had since yellowed, masking Sargent's subtle treatment of colour and light.

→
***Gassed* in the conservation studio, 2023**
A key factor in *Gassed*'s conservation journey was working with experts in spaces large enough to accommodate the painting. In 2022 it was moved to Phil Young's conservation studio to undergo a year-long process of work.

CONSERVING THE PAINTING: PHIL YOUNG, PHILIP YOUNG PAINTINGS CONSERVATION

'The opportunity to conserve *Gassed* was an unusual one. A full restoration involving varnish removal and structural work, addressing underlying supports of the painting and the means by which it is stretched and presented, is a rare event in any institution. My work on paintings by Sargent in the collections at Tate and the National Gallery in Washington D. C. had been limited to minor conservation interventions.

In addition, *Gassed* is not in any way a typical or representative painting by Sargent. It is on an abnormally large scale and as far as we know was completed in a short space of time relative to its size. For *Gassed*, Sargent had to adjust his approach not only to image-making but also to how the painting was made and the paint applied. In addition, he had to consider how such a large format could be constructed to be consistent and balanced. For example, we see quite heavily textured paint (*impasto*) in the sky areas of *Gassed*; this is

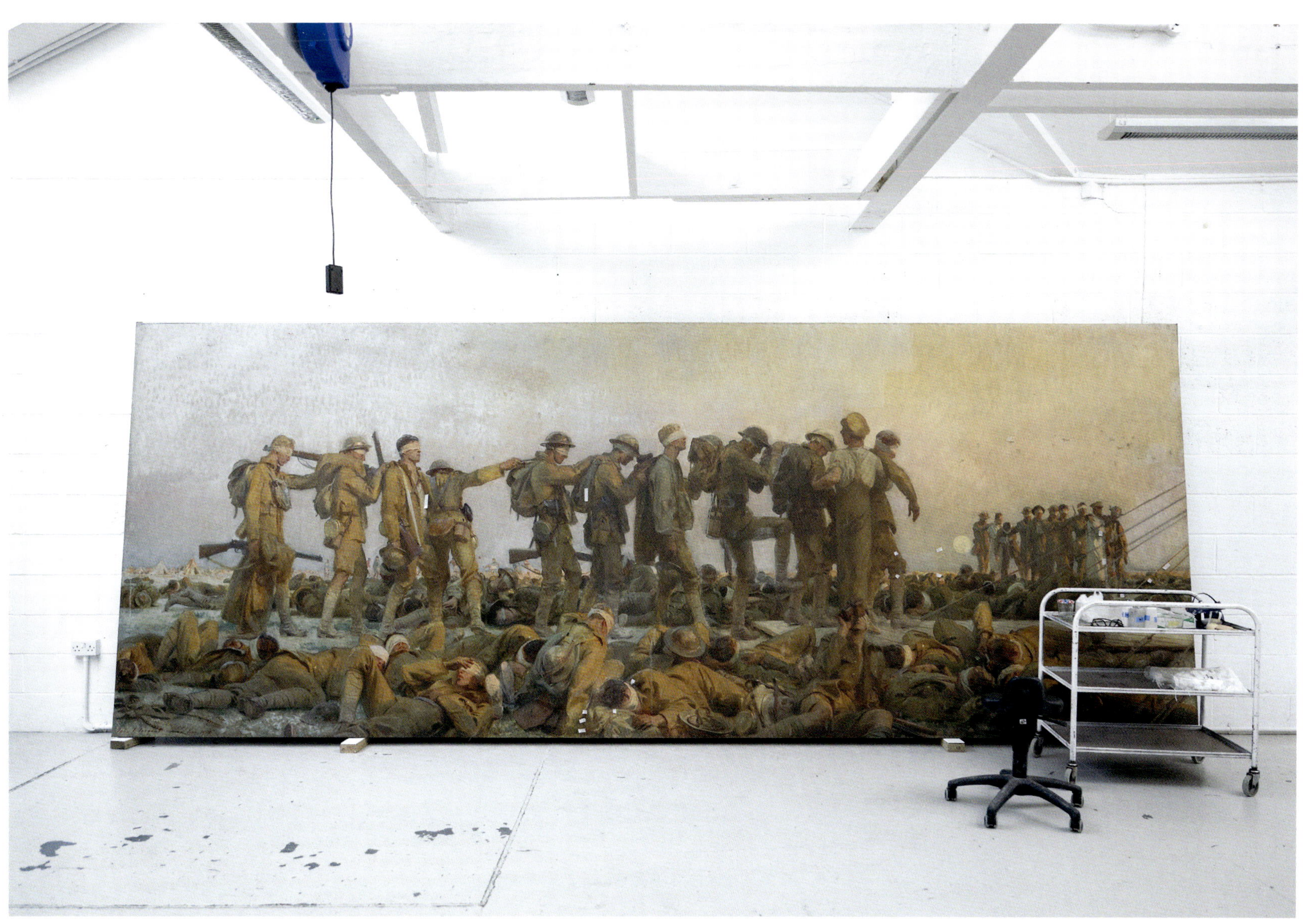

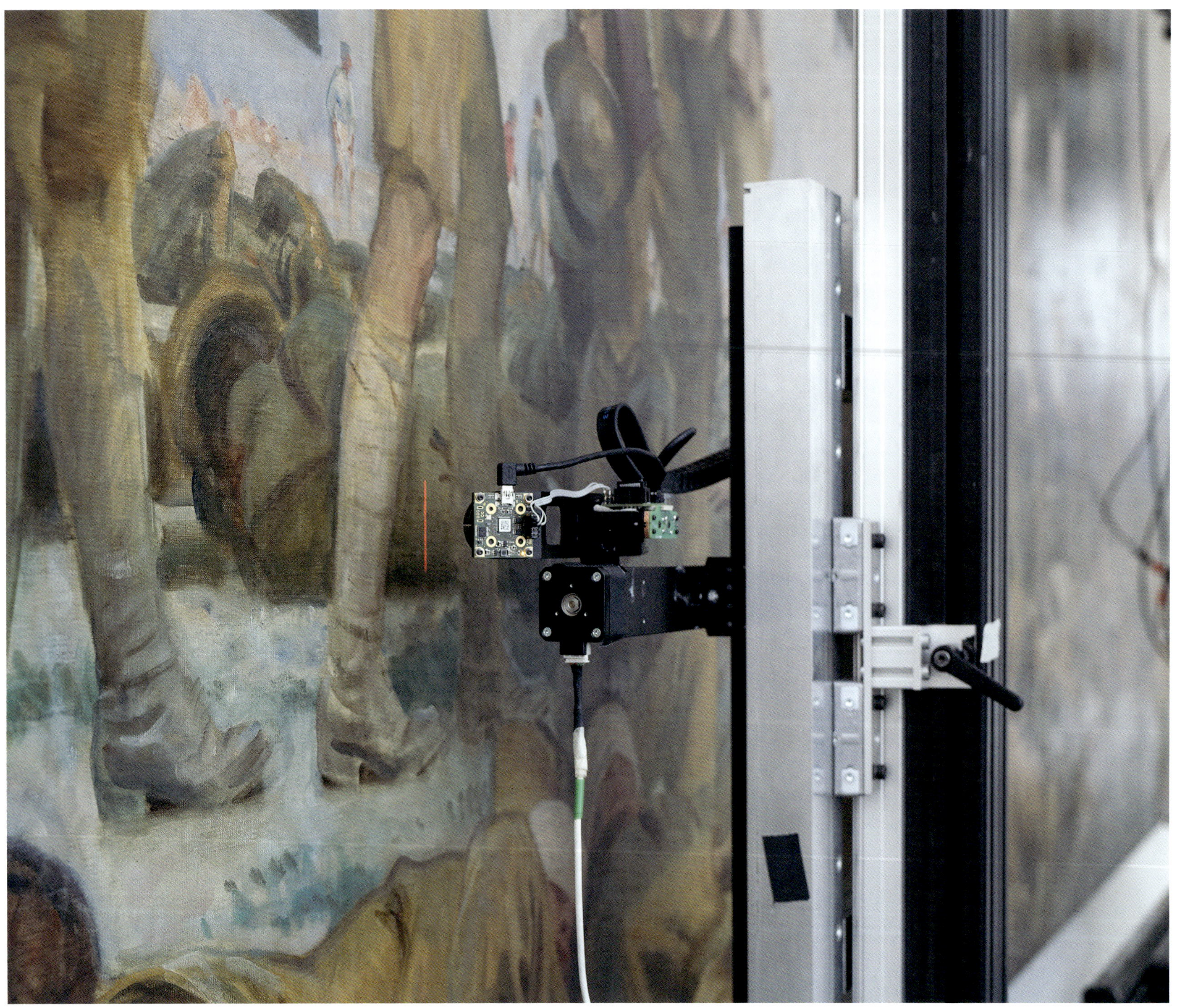

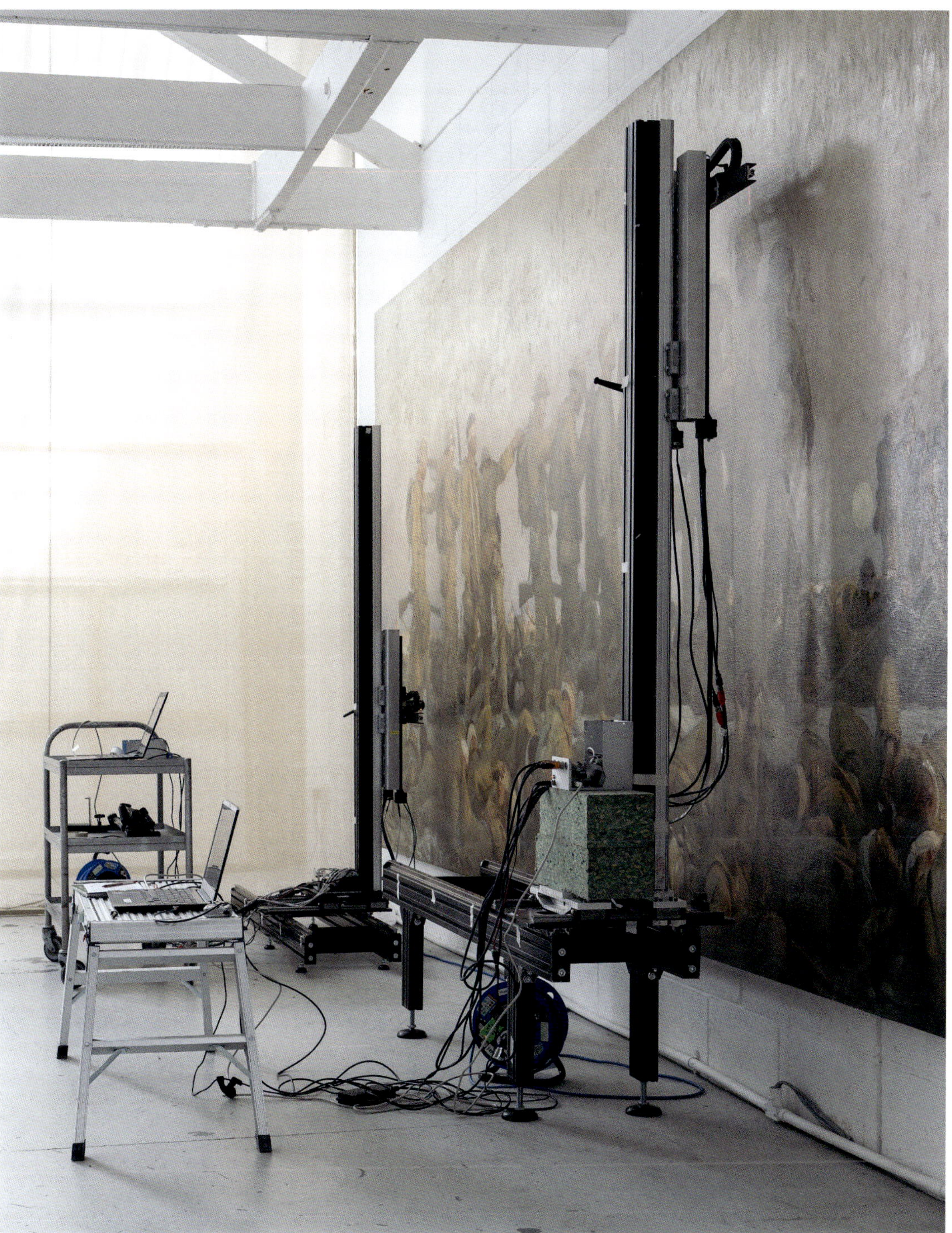

←→

Factum Foundation technology performing 3D scanning of *Gassed*, 2023

As part of the conservation programme, Factum undertook extensive three-dimensional scanning of *Gassed*. The benefits of this are two-fold: access and preservation. Cutting-edge scanning technology produces imaging at the highest possible resolution, meaning the work can be shared with audiences digitally as never before – so extending its reach and impact. Recording the painting in three dimensions, including details of its form and surface modulations to a minute degree, helps us to understand Sargent's practice; it also secures valuable data about the painting for the future.

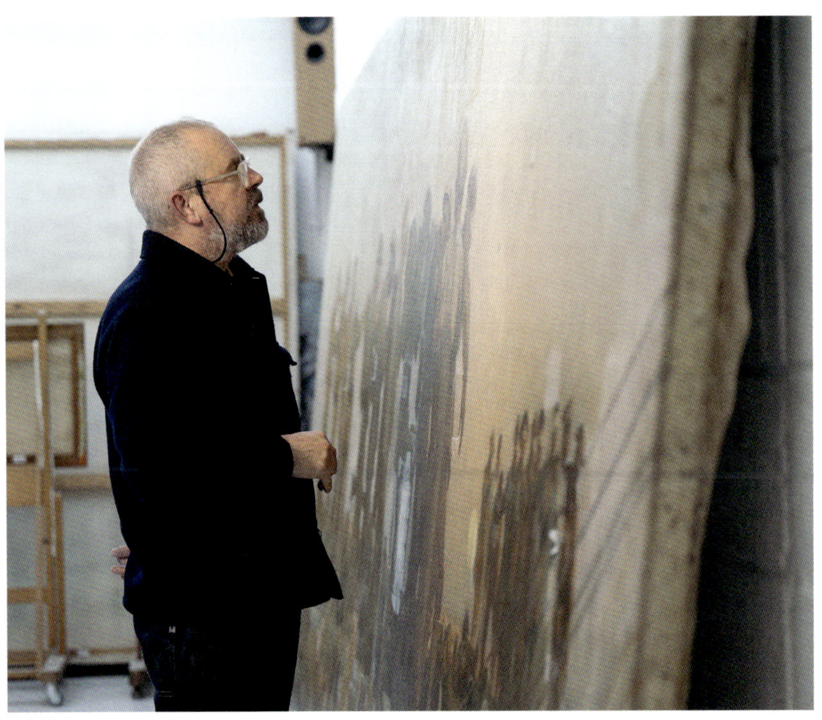

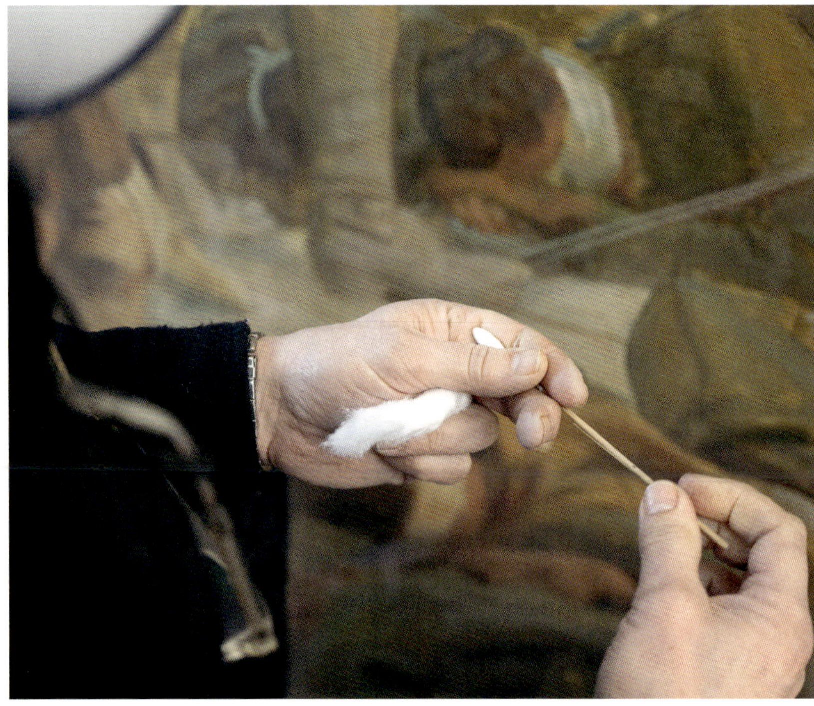

applied broadly and Impressionistically, often in single strong gestures – a very different technique to his highly worked portraits. The canvas is by necessity a thicker and stronger weave, able to withstand the rigours of such strong brushwork and extended scale.

All through my work on this painting I had a feeling of the artist constantly stepping back to take in the broad composition. I could imagine him adding or removing paint and editing the image to be consistent and natural, a very difficult process. The figures are generally painted in flat paint with a high oil content, but on close examination they seem in many cases to be sketched in paint (such as the figure on the ground at the far right of the painting). The many visible revisions in composition (*pentimenti*) which show through attest to this and demonstrate Sargent's fluency and skill in painting.

Documented in archives at Tate, we know that Sargent regularly changed details in his compositions, often quite boldly; he even scraped back whole areas painted the day before, while the oil paint remained wet. In the case of *Gassed*, *pentimenti* show through where he made

↖
Conservator Phil Young inspects *Gassed* in his conservation studio, 2023
For Phil Young, close inspection of the painting yielded significant information. Through initial visual examination, for example, it was clear that the yellow varnish layers passed over previous restoration and retouchings, and filled losses and structural repairs to the canvas. Interestingly some of Sargent's changes during painting – known as *pentimenti* – are clearly evident to the naked eye.

↑→
Conservator Phil Young cleaning *Gassed*, 2023
Cleaning and solubility tests were used during the examination of *Gassed* to understand its construction and the nature of the yellowed varnish layers. Both newer modern resin and natural resin varnishes were detected in this process.

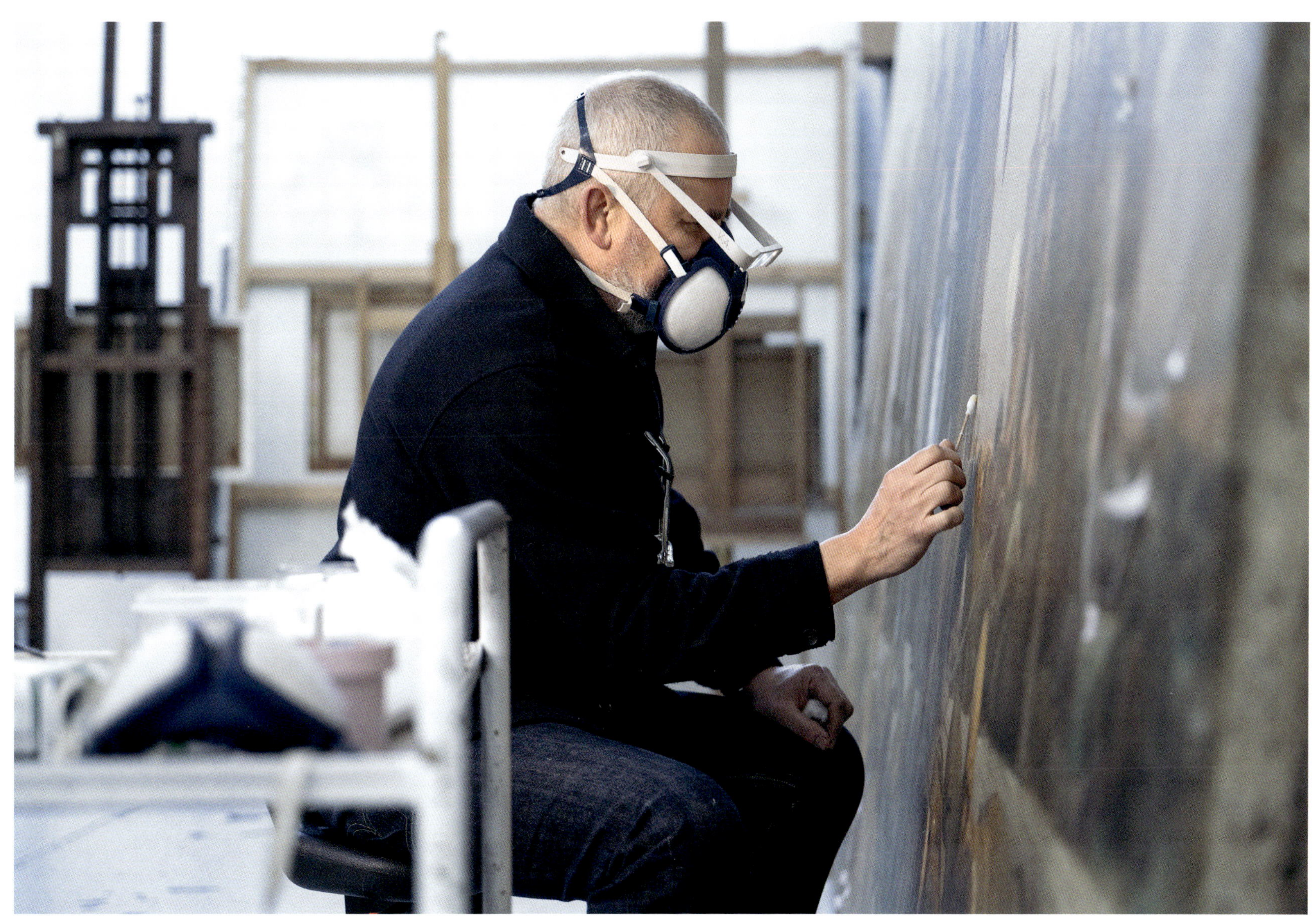

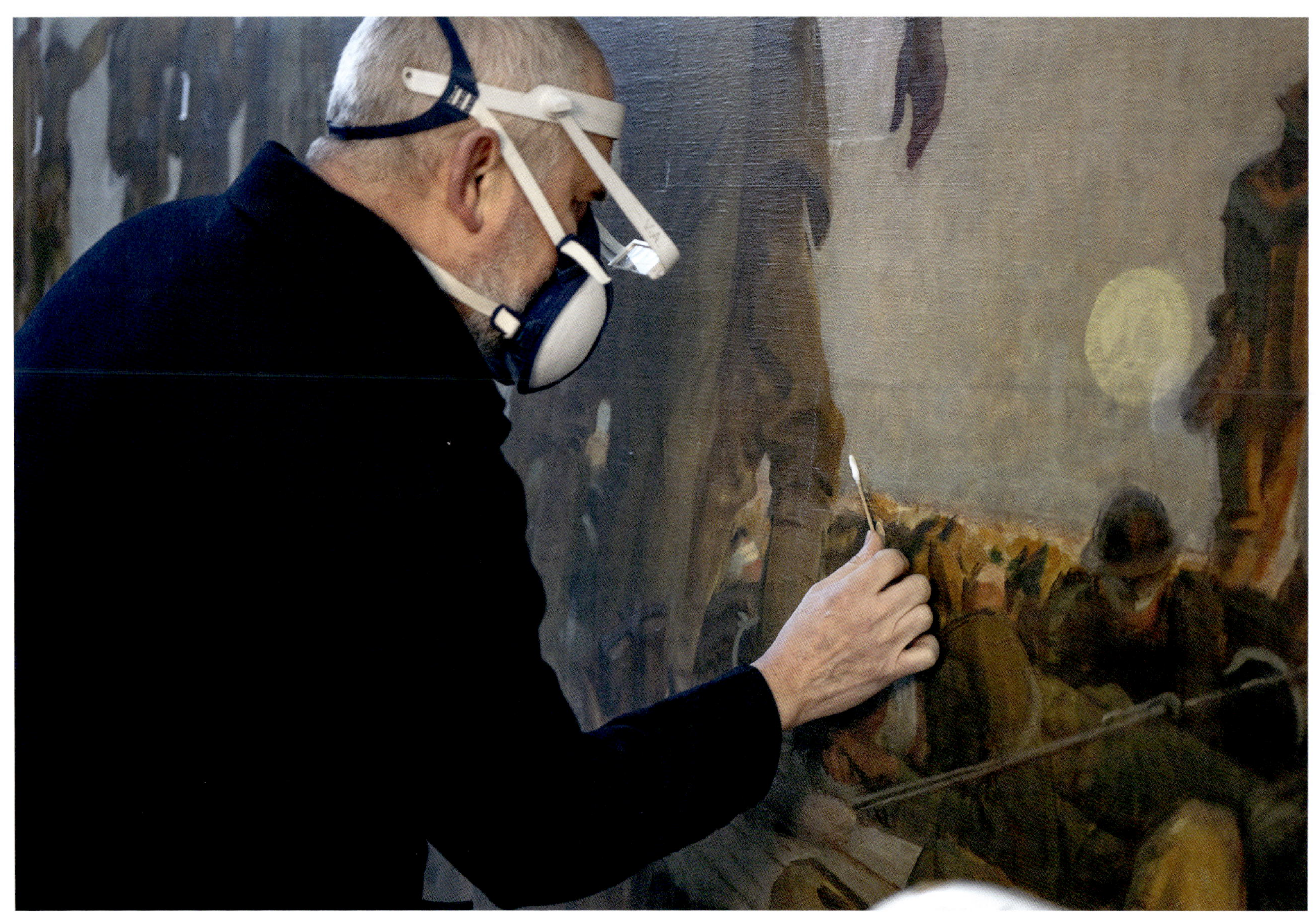

↑
Conservator Phil Young cleaning *Gassed*, 2023
Phil Young's meticulous cleaning of *Gassed* was a slow and painstaking task. He used gentle solvents and methodical techniques in the conservation process, passing over the whole painting twice.

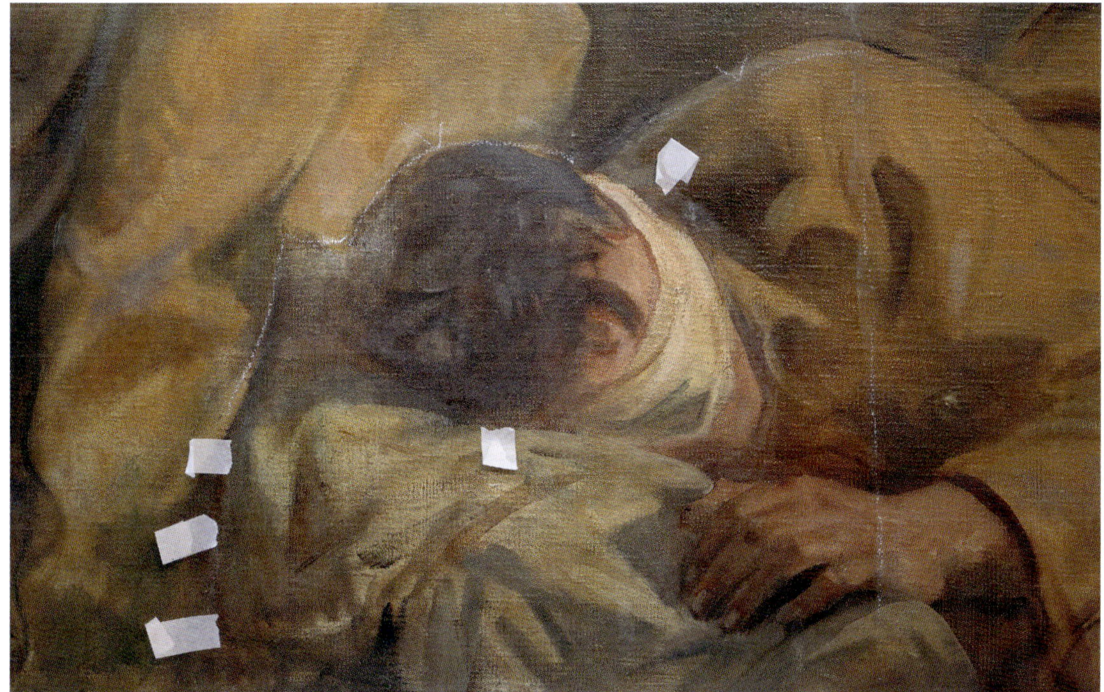

←

Detail of *Gassed* with low-tack tape markers to indicate cleaned area, 2023

Gassed had two full cleans between 2022 and 2023. The first removed a grey-yellow layer which included surface dirt and the second lifted off a layer of yellowed historical varnish. Cleaning tests areas were distributed across the canvas to see their effect on differing parts of the painting. Removal of the old varnish revealed the clarity and saturation of Sargent's colours: the pinks, blues, greens and yellow in the sky area are richer and the details of khaki unforms crisper. Light and dark across the painting are more highly contrasted.

alterations to already dry areas, thus several weeks or months after painting. It is likely that he continued to tweak the figure positions, the angles of the guns, the heads and helmets as the whole image developed, or even possibly all together at the end. Often *pentimenti* show through more with age, but some areas of Sargent's tweaking are so clear that they must always have been apparent – possibly indicating that he was pressed for time and needed to adapt his methodology accordingly. The position of the moon, for instance, seems to have changed many times, probably as Sargent worked out how to represent the sunset in the scene. It started on the far right, then occupied four or five positions above and slightly to the right of where the moon appears in the finished painting. The perfectly circular alterations and painted-over areas are clear to see.

Given the scale and age of *Gassed*, its condition is extraordinarily good. Because it is the largest painting in the IWM collection, its movements and exposure have been restricted, meaning that there are just two or three minor pieces of canvas damage and scattered patches of restoration – no large tears or gaping holes that we might expect to see in another context. Some wear and tear has occurred around the edges, due to the painting being rolled and unrolled a number of times. As *Gassed* has been on near-constant view since arrival at IWM, there has until now been little chance for a more sustained programme of conservation. Restoration in the mid-1970s involved changing the stretcher and varnish, removing dirt and revarnishing the painting. Since then there have been only small interventions to address scratches on top of that work.

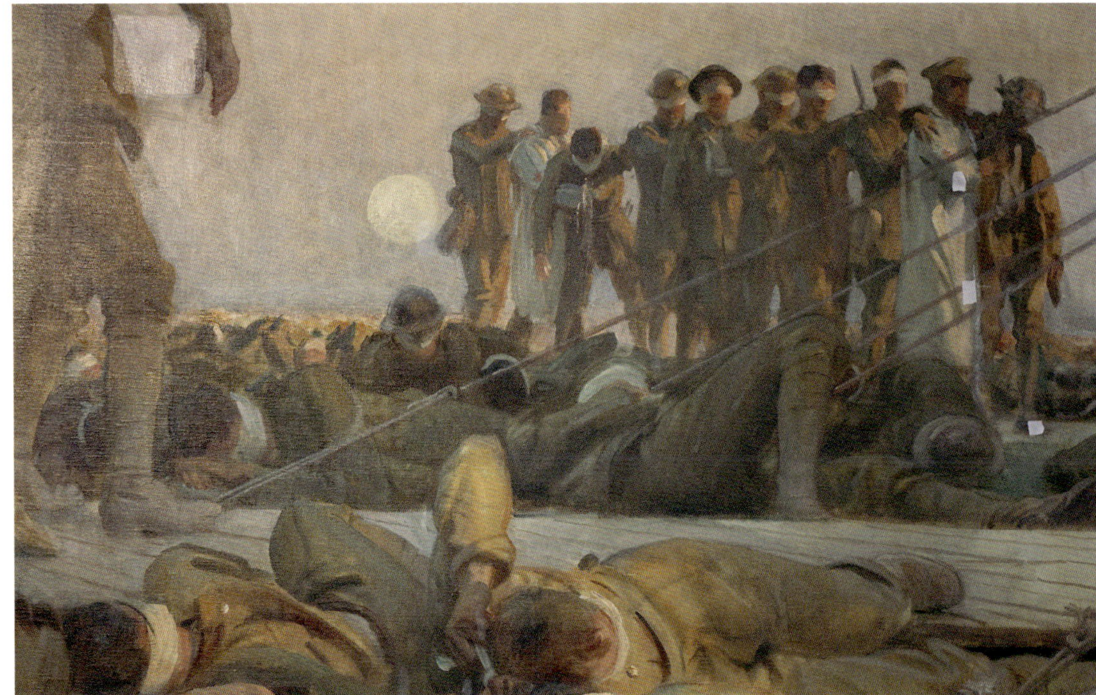

←

Detail of *Gassed* with cleaning patch test visible at top edge, 2023

Cleaning undertaken during conservation revealed intriguing details of Sargent's technique and process. Removing dirt and layers of yellowed varnish with gentle solvents showed the artist's colour choices, adjustments and amendments more clearly. The moon, for instance, was initially on the far right of the painting. As the composition evolved, the moon appeared in various positions above and slightly to the right of its eventual location.

As is the case with other works by Sargent, we know that *Gassed* was not varnished in Sargent's lifetime; indeed, it was probably not varnished until the very late 1920s or early 1930s. In approaching conservation of the painting, then, the starting premise was that any varnish present was added significantly later. The varnish applied during the restoration in the 1970s was used thickly and was of a type that has yellowed dramatically over the decades since. On dark paintings this gradual effect is less noticeable. It seems that viewers had grown used to seeing *Gassed* as a yellow painting, when in fact is it a compositionally bright and colourful record of a hot summer's evening during the artist's visit to France in 1918. Sargent's use of colour is well-known and often spectacular, a feature that had been concealed in later years by the discoloured varnish.

Ultraviolet light can help to determine that layers or areas of restoration have been applied at different times, without being able to date them accurately. Through the use of ultraviolet light, we could perceive several ages of retouching. This addressed scratches and small paint losses, some below the varnish, others on top and some very old. Cleaning and solubility tests were carried out to learn about the nature of the varnish layers and to investigate how they could best be removed. Through examination alone, however, it became clear that the yellow varnish layers passed over previous restoration, retouchings and filled losses; they went over structural repairs to the canvas. Combined with documentary evidence that the painting was not varnished by the artist, it was clear that the main varnish layers were not original; they had been retrospectively applied.

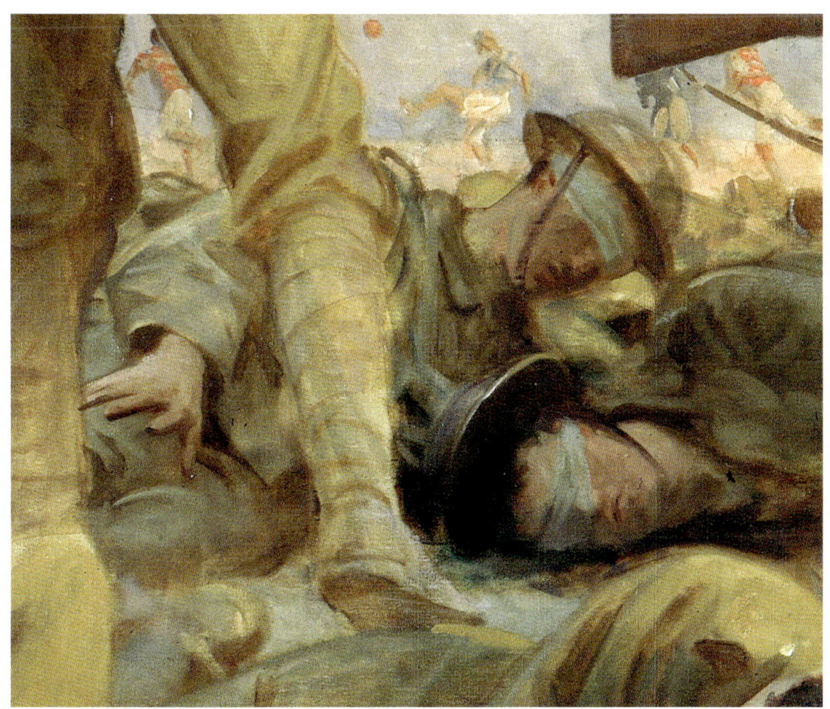

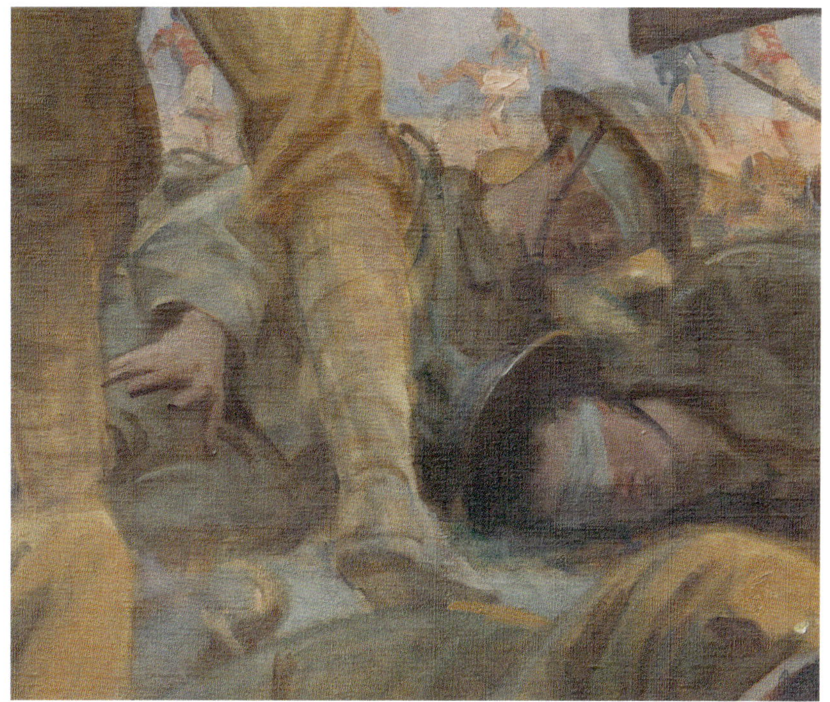

↑

Pre- and post-conservation details of John Singer Sargent, *Gassed*, with bandaged figure, 1919

OIL ON CANVAS

Sargent did not typically varnish his paintings and he did not varnish *Gassed*. The painting is Impressionistic and surprisingly gestural in places. Its composition – the central line of soldiers linked by arms and legs – relies on windows of contrast between the drab khaki of their uniforms, leading down into the foreground mass of intermingled bodies and the bright sunset sky, lit by a pale moon. Methodical cleaning of *Gassed*, especially the removal of old varnish, has revealed Sargent's fresh brushwork to show careful use of blues, pinks and greens.

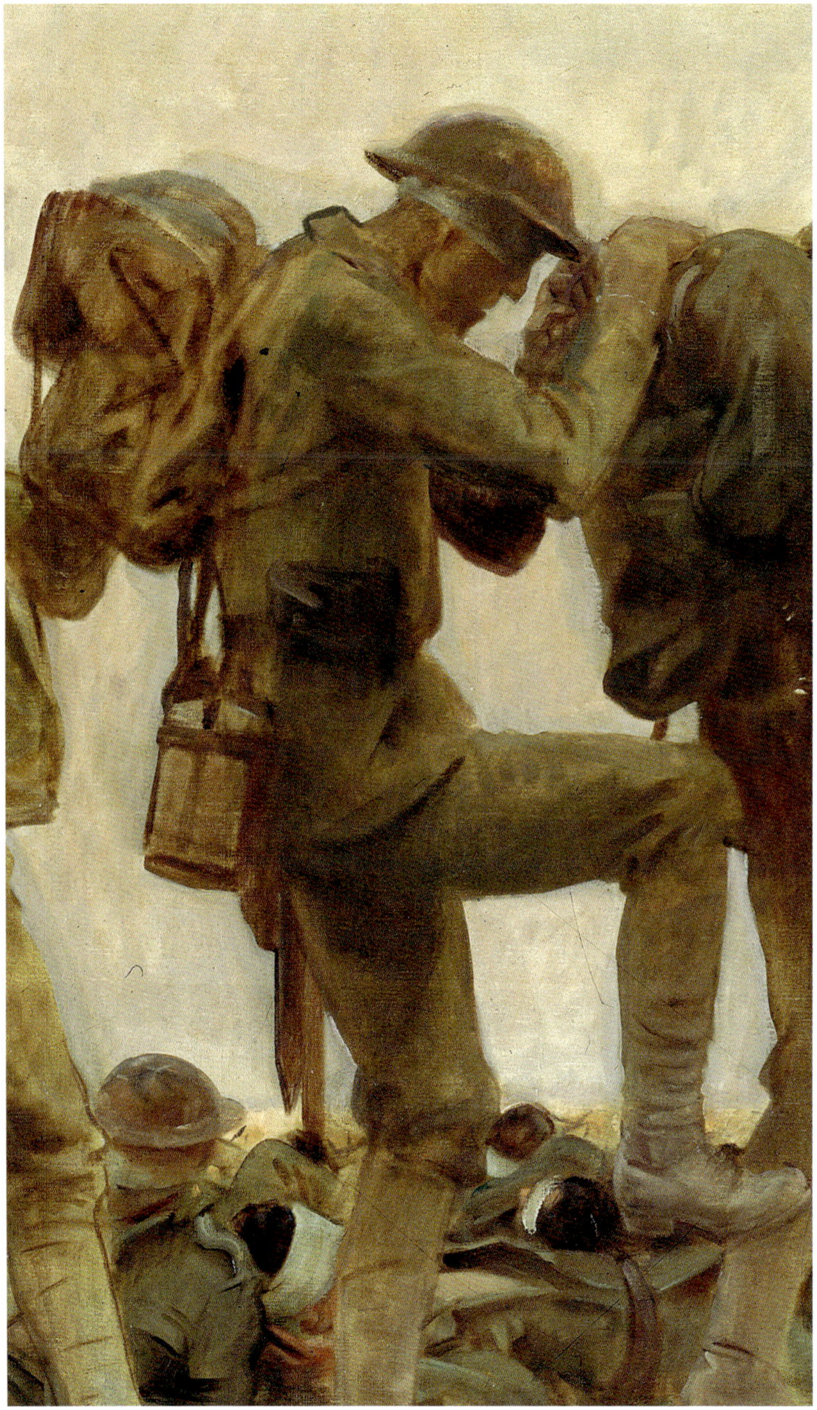

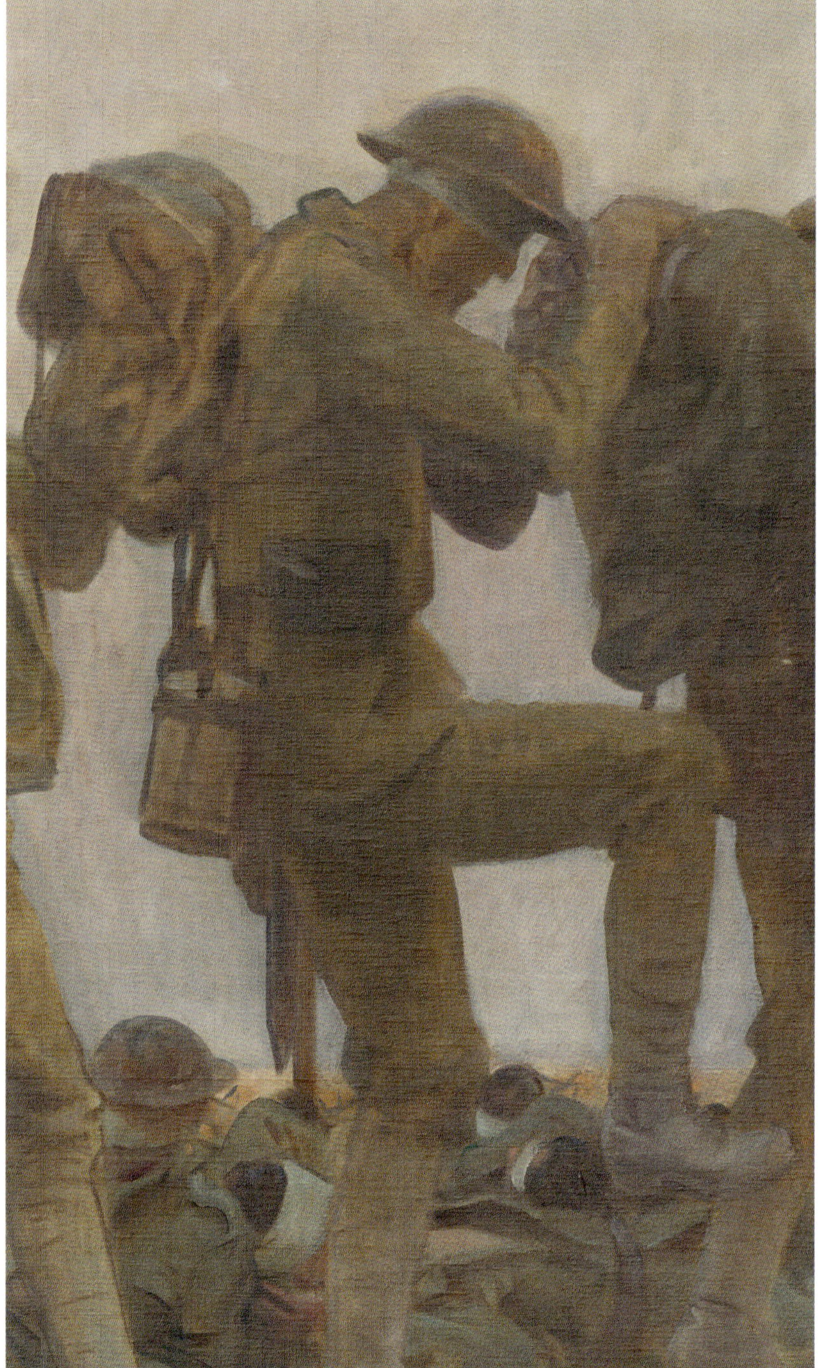

←

Pre- and post-conservation details of John Singer Sargent, *Gassed*, showing figure with bent leg, 1919

OIL ON CANVAS

Surgeon and fellow artist Henry Tonks described the scene for *Gassed* which had so interested Sargent as 'a very fine evening and the sun toward setting'. Sargent's watercolours in France similarly depict a colourful environment full of blue, pink and lilac – colours obscured in *Gassed* by decades of varnish discolouration. Conservation has now restored the scene's original freshness and coherence.

Cleaning away the yellowed varnish layers from the painting was to prove a revelation. Gradually I saw the soft and subtle pinks, yellows and greens in the sky (reminiscent of work by Sargent's friend Claude Monet) emerge, and the soft outline of the soldiers against the setting sun, almost self-illuminating, also became apparent. The three-dimensionality of the view, including the footballers in the distance, also developed with the cleaning. Previously the darkened varnish and dirt layers had flattened the image visually.

As tests progressed, we discovered that there were remnants of an earlier varnish, this time a natural resin, caught in the heavy texture of the sky. Possibly dating from the 1930s, it appears this varnish was removed in the 1970s (the reports at the time describe doing so), but not entirely – a fact that partly accounted for the uneven yellowness of the sky in particular. Caught in this varnish were large clumps of cotton wool from a rather hurried cleaning process – according to the records, the cleaning in the 1970s was competed in a matter of days, compared with the six months I took to remove all the subsequent layers. A new varnish has been applied that, as far as we know, will not discolour, the plan from the outset being to use as little varnish as possible to allow variations in the texture of brushstrokes to be evident. Critically, everything applied in the conservation process this time is reversible.

The scale of the painting has also been a factor in unpicking interventions from the past and in creating a stable future for the painting. In the 1980s *Gassed* was strip-lined, a process in which a reinforcing canvas is attached to the edges of the painting to strengthen and stiffen crucial areas. This made stretching the canvas difficult,

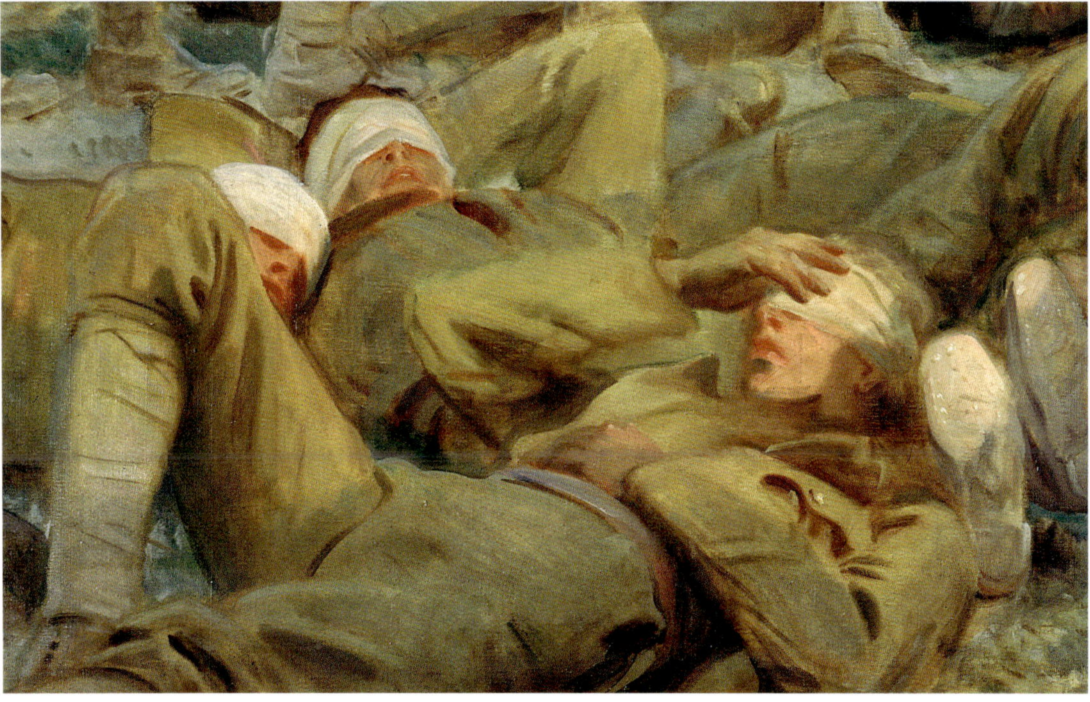

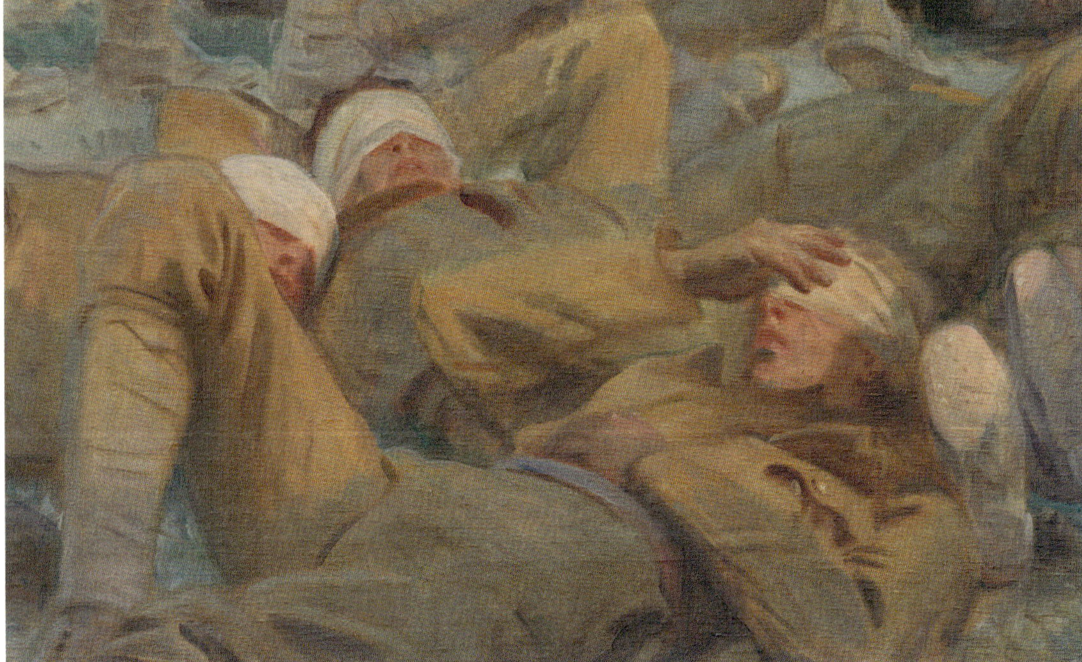

←

Pre- and post-conservation details of John Singer Sargent, *Gassed*, with reclined gassed victim, 1919

OIL ON CANVAS

The tightly interwoven huddle of bodies pressed up against the picture plane in the foreground of *Gassed* is vital to its composition and meaning. Sargent used bursts of colour to pick out the bodies of gassed cases – all propped elbows and bent knees – against the ground. The subtleties of the men's white bandages, the green grass beneath them, their skin tones and uniforms had all been flattened by the overly-yellow hue of old varnish. Conservation has revealed their original freshness and distinction.

→

Pre- and post-conservation details of John Singer Sargent, *Gassed*, with bowed figure, 1919

OIL ON CANVAS

Details of soldiers' uniform have become more apparent with the cleaning of *Gassed* during the conservation work. Colour was very important in Sargent's Impressionistic practice. As shown in this detail, he used green and blue to pick out the lid and strap of the soldier's water bottle, pack, eye bandage and arm crease.

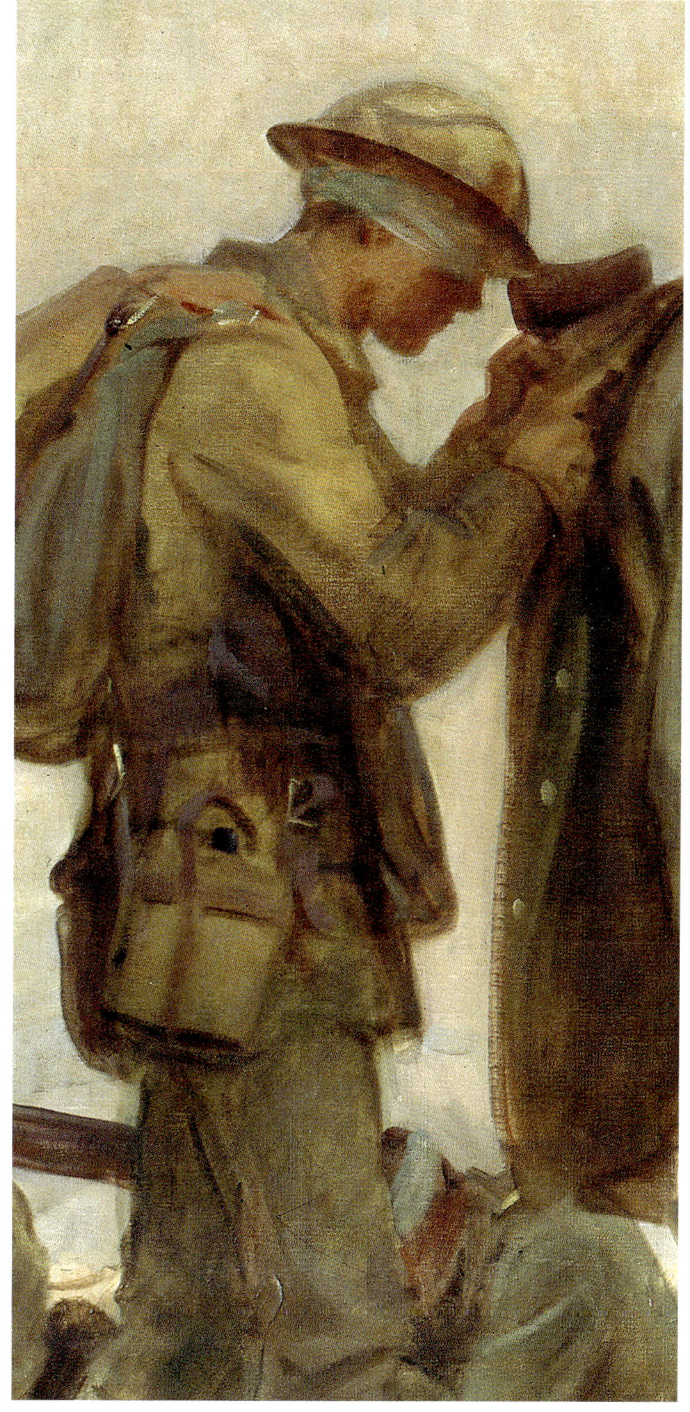

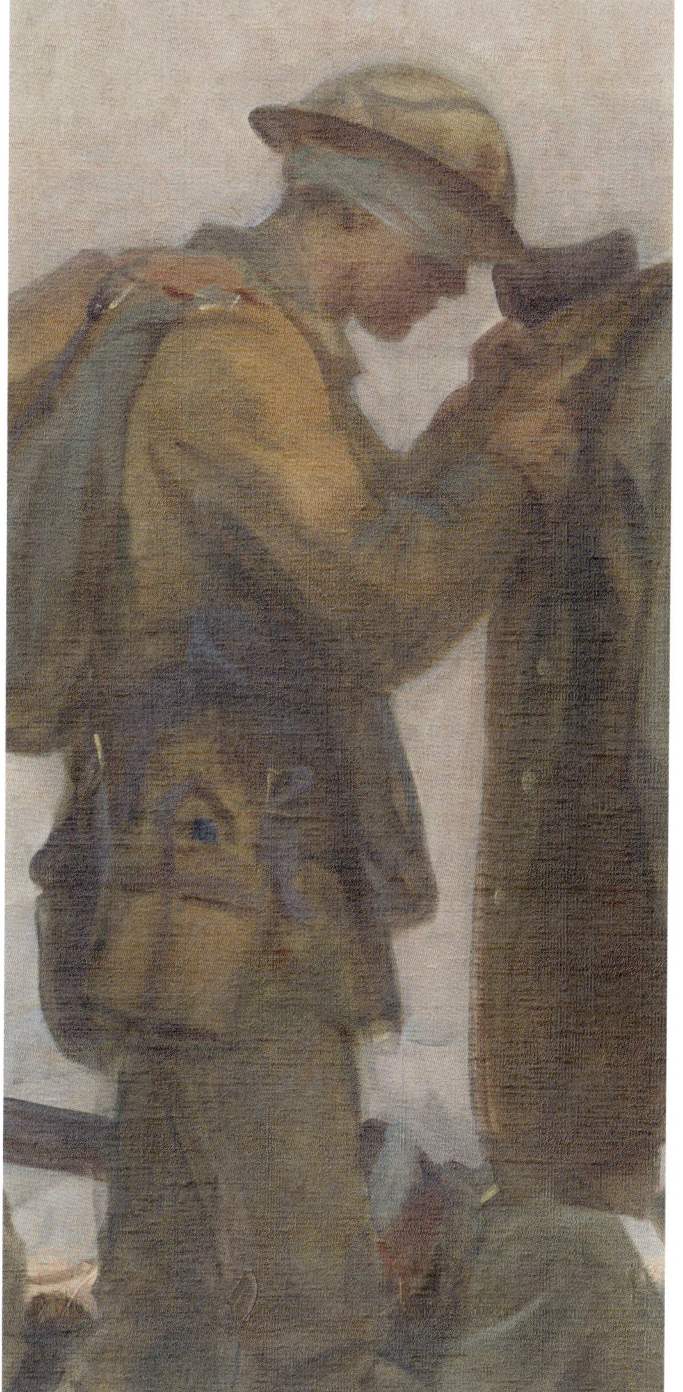

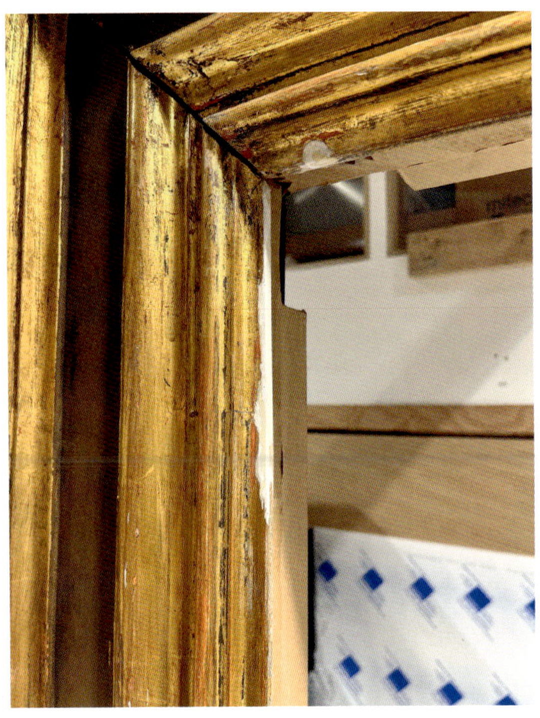

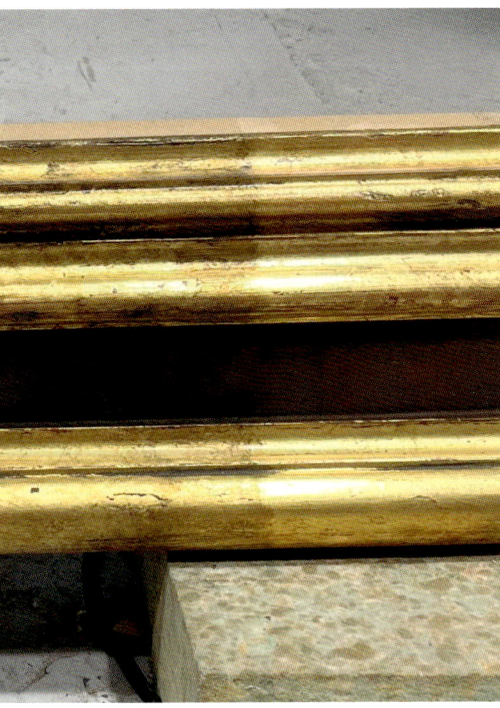

←

Two views of the frame of *Gassed* before conservation, 2023

Hans Thompson of Orbis Conservation undertook analysis and treatment of the frame of *Gassed*. Tests showed that treatment of the frame in the 1970s had resulted in an over-bright gold finish; vivid orange bole had been applied at the same time. The frame required toning to achieve a more sympathetic finish, closer to the original scheme.

leaving it prone to bulging and warping. In addition, the stretcher used in the mid-1970s was metal and not quite the right size. Together these factors meant that when hung, *Gassed* distorted under the weight of the stretcher and frame. The structural work to address these issues, like the cleaning, needed to be thorough and methodical. A new aluminium and plywood stretcher, made to match the size of the image, revealed Sargent's signature in full once again. It had been cut horizontally through the middle in the old construction of stretcher and frame.

Working with Orbis Conservation while undertaking conservation of the painting, we knew from the outset that a new hanging system for the painting and the frame would be required. This would prevent any distortion and would stop the painting and frame being subject to the weight of each other. In a step that ensures a long life for each part of the whole, they now are installed independently. *Gassed* is not a painting typical of the early twentieth century – flat and shiny, perhaps dark and heavily saturated. Instead it is a freely painted, large format image which compelled the artist to adjust his technique to the task and the scale. I reproduced this approach when taking it on as conservator.'

CONSERVING THE FRAME: HANS THOMPSON, ORBIS CONSERVATION

'The frame for *Gassed* has a fascinating history. Archival records on British frame makers from the National Portrait Gallery note that several framers were working with both Sargent and various national institutions during the early twentieth century, including the Royal Academy. Perhaps the most likely manufacturer of the *Gassed* frame was

→

Analysis of the frame of *Gassed*, 2023
The opportunity to carry out conservation work on both painting and frame was very valuable to those involved. Here Phil Young meets with the Orbis Conservation team to discuss aspects of the project.

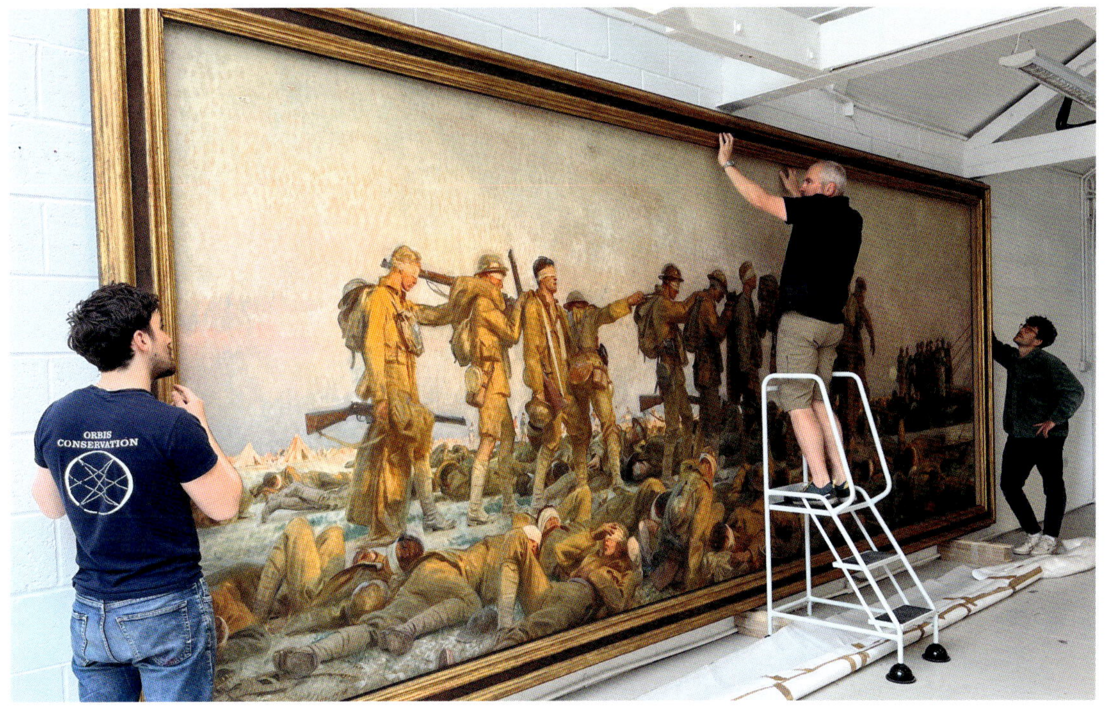

Charles Mitchell May. Known to have ties with both the Royal Academy and the IWM, May was also working closely with Sargent between 1894 and 1922, most regularly on his Royal Academy exhibits. This and the fact that May & Son were part of an effort to frame the work of war artists during and after the First World War – notably providing 'details of a frame in 1919' to the IWM – suggest that he designed this monumental frame for the artist. Another painting of a similar scale by Sargent, *General Officers of World War One*, 1919–1922, now in the National Portrait Gallery, was framed by Mitchell May and contains the same wide, flat central frieze.

When the *Gassed* frame arrived at the Orbis Conservation workshop, it was important to establish – through sampling and microscope analysis – whether its current decorative scheme was original or had

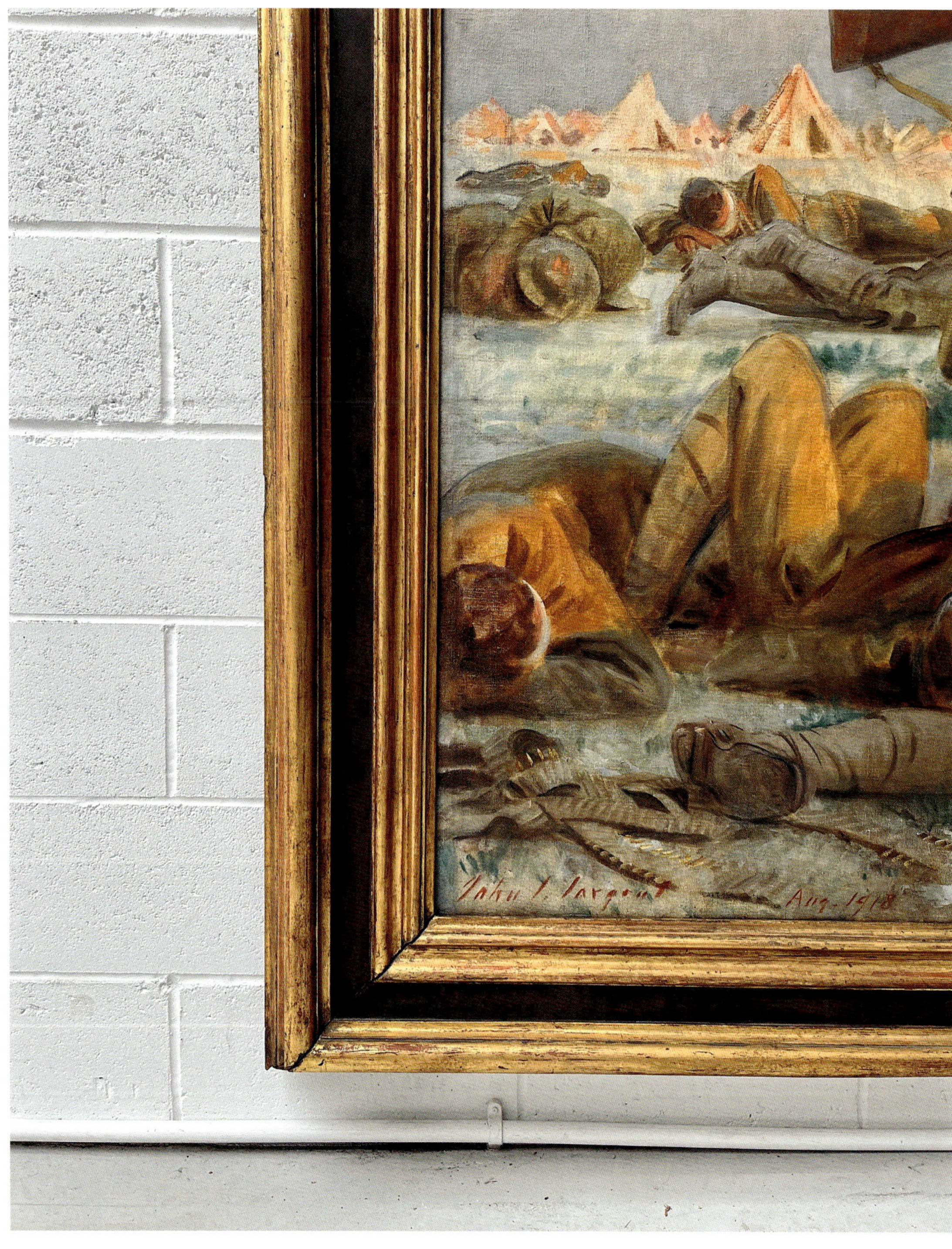

←

Detail of *Gassed*, showing newly conserved frame, 2023
Sargent recognised the importance of frames in presenting his work and worked closely with framers to realise his vision. Following specialist treatment from Orbis Conservation, the frame once again complements *Gassed* as the artist would have wished. Sargent's signature is also once again clearly visible.

→→

***Gassed* arrives back at IWM London following conservation work, July 2023**
Following conservation work, *Gassed* has become the centrepiece of the Blavatnik Art, Film and Photography Galleries at IWM London. Prior to the opening of the galleries on 10 November 2023, specialist art handling teams craned the huge painting through the IWM London building. The monumental scale of *Gassed* means that routes through the building must be meticulously planned in advance.

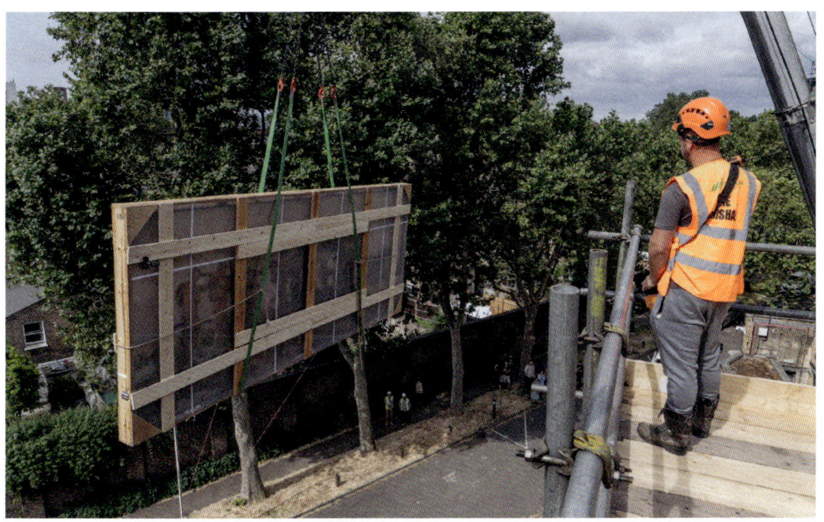

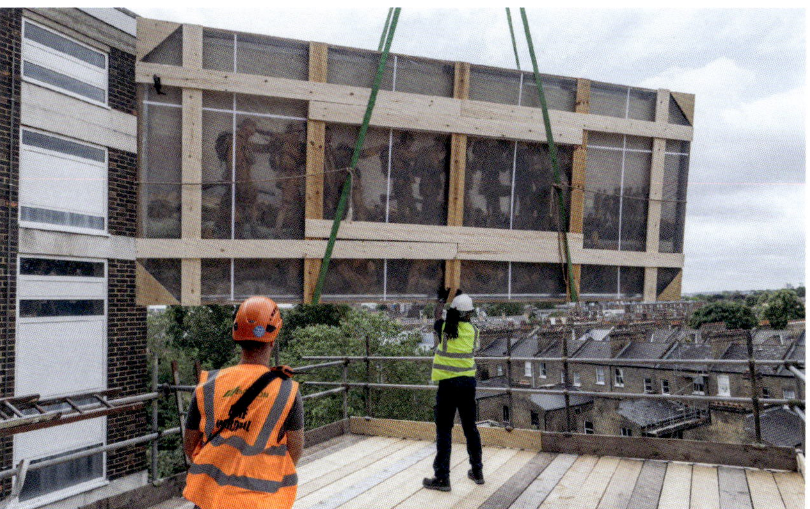

been shaped by regilding or repainting at some point in its history. Analysis revealed that the frame had probably been stripped of its original scheme and redecorated several times during its life, most likely when the painting was restored in the 1970s. The frame's visual appearance confirmed what analysis had indicated: both the vivid orange bole (an underlayer made of fine, richly-coloured clay mixed with water and glue) used widely during the 1970s and the bright, golden gild seemed at odds with archival images of *Gassed*. These included the famous photograph of the painting on display at Crystal Palace in 1921 (*see pages 32 and 61*), which shows the frame with a matte, muted finish. Orbis undertook to achieve a more sympathetic finish that would bring the experience of the painting closer to the way it would have originally been seen. The treatment was carried out in four stages: cleaning, removing unsatisfactory historic repairs, consolidation of gilding, and toning and distressing. Each step was completed before undertaking the next stage. After dry cleaning, bright areas of clumsily applied paint were removed, areas of loss and lifted gilding were repaired and the whole frame was toned down.

During the process of frame conservation, we kept close contact during the cleaning of the painting and its progress. A priority was to ensure that, when treated, both the frame and the painting were in harmony, something that had not been the case over the past few decades. Research showed that such a pairing of frame and painting was significant to Sargent. That he commissioned painting-specific frames was not unusual, but the artist's level of dedication to his frames and clients was unique. Evidence of this concern has been described as 'three-fold: correspondence with his patrons, the recurrence of certain favoured frame patterns and the survival of various frames labelled by one or another of his favoured frame makers'.[23] Following treatment, the frame and painting were reunited; no longer in conflict, they complemented one another. As a result, we now see more closely the character of *Gassed* as it appeared when first unveiled to its public.'

WAR ARTISTS AND CONTEMPORARY CONFLICT

The Blavatnik Art, Film and Photography Galleries provide a vivid and intriguing setting for *Gassed*. They enable the painting to enter

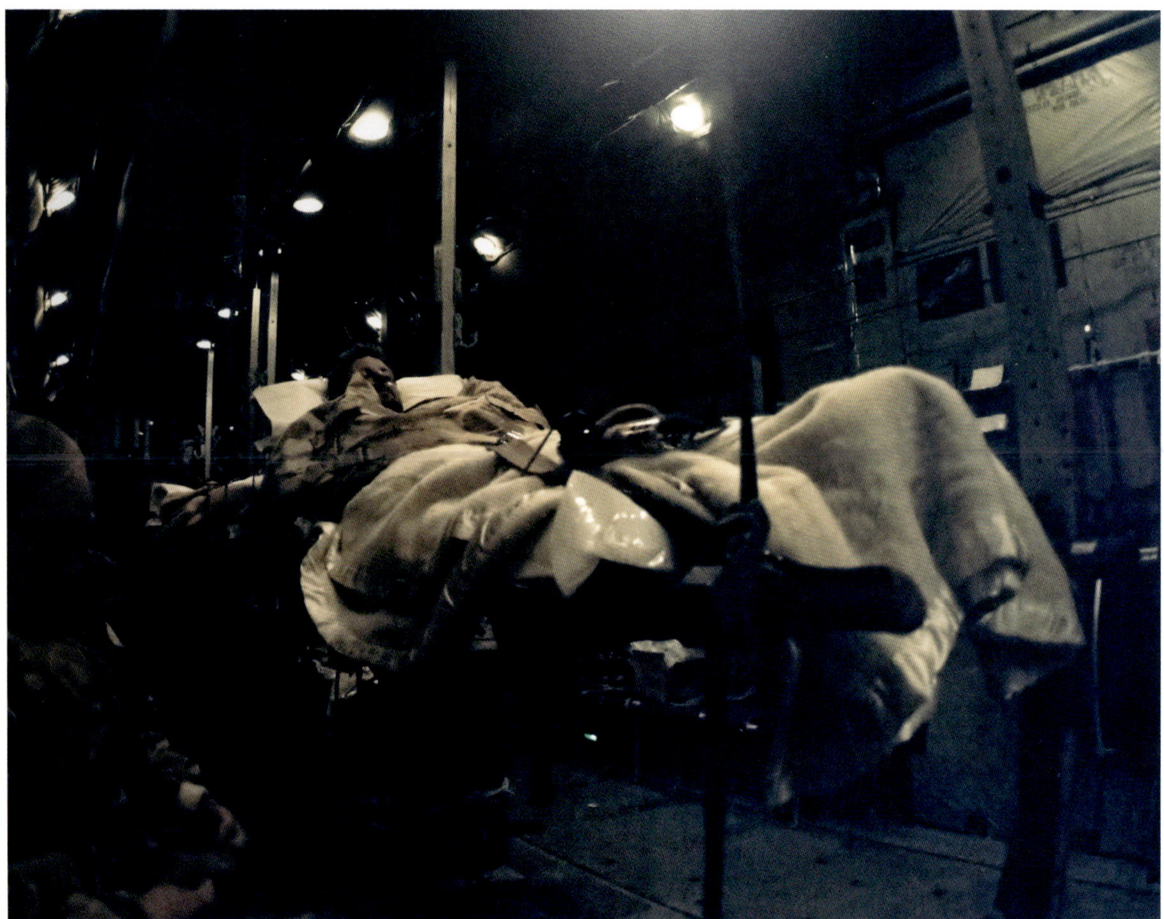

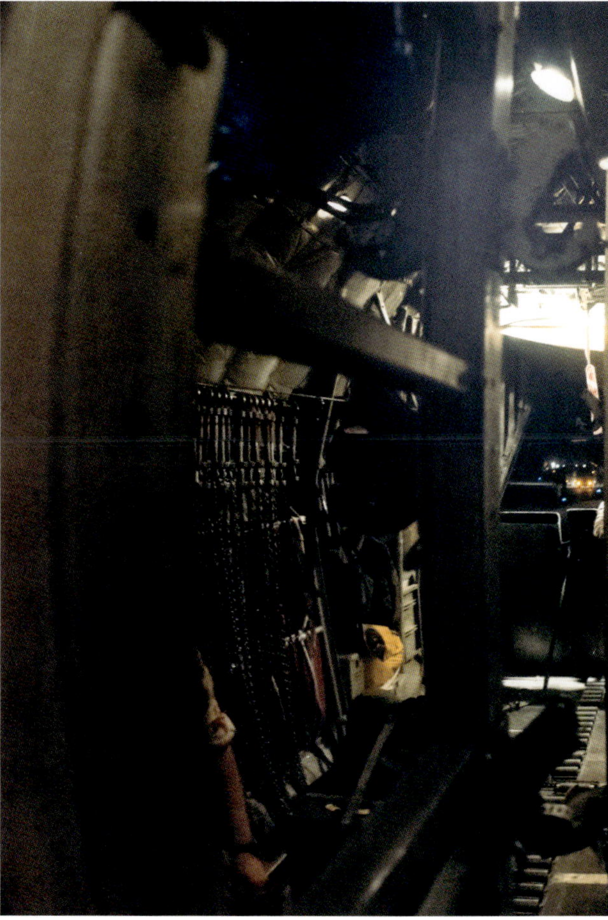

into new and powerful dialogue with artists, photographers and filmmakers who have continued to engage with the enduring themes and experiences of conflict. More than a century since *Gassed* was made, contemporary artists continue to have a special role in documenting medical responses on the front line, complementing the painting's impact and legacy.

Two of those artists, David Cotterrell and Tim Hetherington, deal directly with consciousness, suffering and sight. In so doing, they demonstrate the thematic and practical continuities and differences of practice since Sargent's day. As in the encounter of Sargent's commission, practitioners today still grapple with complex narrative challenges in diverse ethical, political and cultural contexts, as well as with the central problem of representing the unrepresentable.

In 2007 David Cotterrell was commissioned as a war artist to travel to Camp Bastion in Afghanistan. He spent time embedded with British forces and made a series of photographs about the treatment of wounded soldiers, documenting their journeys back to the UK for further treatment at Selly Oak, Birmingham.

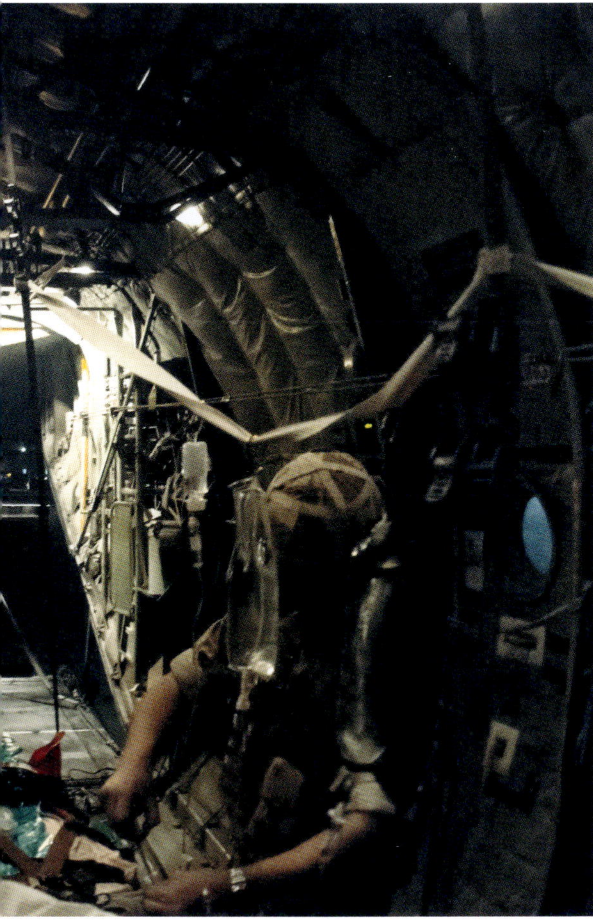

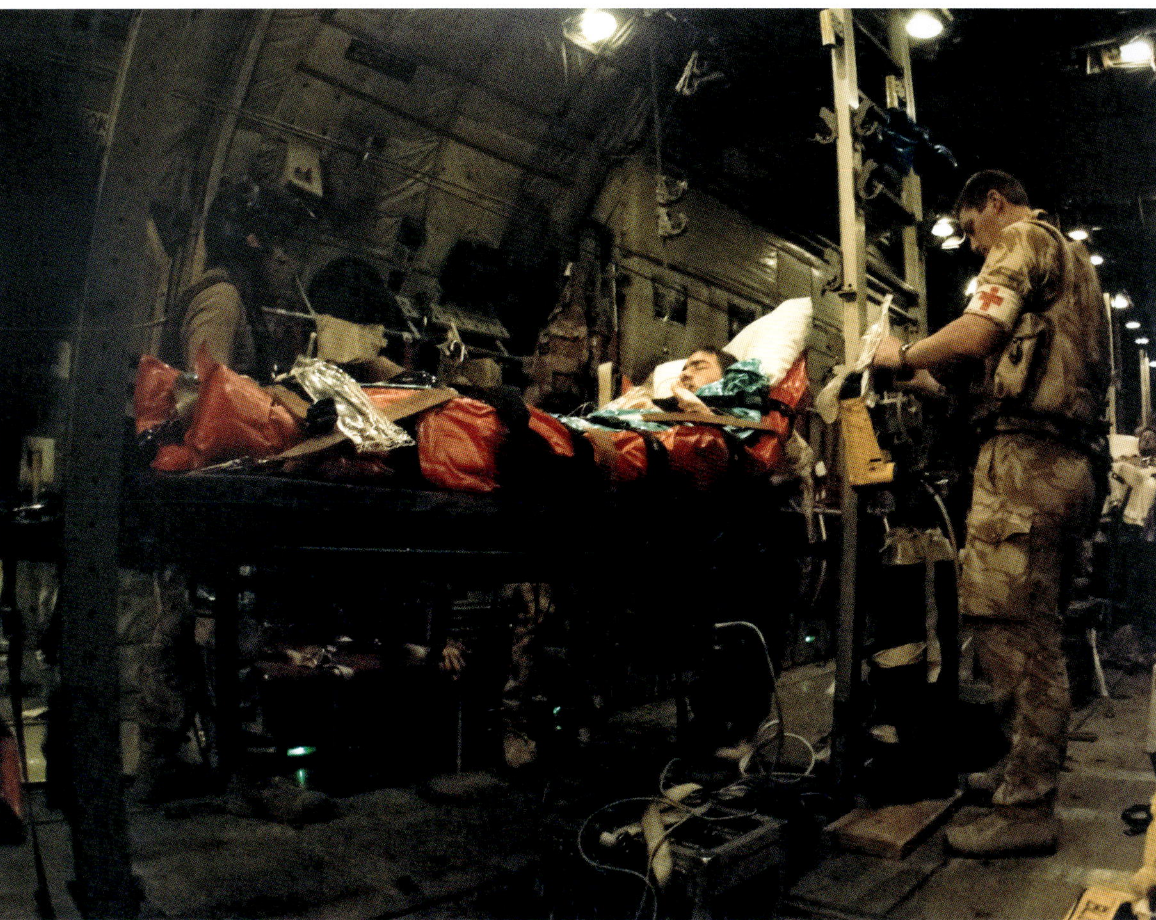

In his work Cotterrell reflected on the 'problematic' nature of taking photographs of injured, unconscious and vulnerable people. Although military personnel had been briefed and consent sought, he was conscious that 'it feels potentially uncomfortable to have images that potentially are beautiful but represent life changing, horrific images in other people's lives'. Cotterrell's project highlighted the ongoing ethical questions faced by artists in capturing sensitive situations in conflict.

Tim Hetherington's *War Blind* series was made during five years spent in Freetown, Sierra Leone. Many of the subjects in the portraits

↑
David Cotterrell, *Gateway II*, 2009

C-TYPE PRINT ON ALUMINIUM

In 2007 David Cotterrell was commissioned to travel to Helmand Province, Afghanistan to observe the work of the medical teams at Camp Bastion, a British Army base. His triptych photographs depict wounded soldiers being moved onto the plane home. Strapped to stretchers, the men appear small and vulnerable in the cavernous space of the aircraft.

were left with serious medical conditions as a consequence of civil war. The fighters of the Revolutionary United Front (RUF) terrorised local populations by removing their eyes. Others lost their sight because of malnutrition or lack of access to healthcare.

In the series Hetherington engaged directly and powerfully with the concept of vision. Light and shadow contrast sharply and one man covers an eye as he looks straight to camera.

CONCLUSION

More than a century after *Gassed* arrived at IWM, the impact of this monumental painting is as strong as ever. New information revealed through conservation has enabled us to see the work again as Sargent intended and to explore themes of suffering and loss, creativity and memorialisation in the context of other war art. In its dominant position in prestigious new galleries, its legacy secured, *Gassed* can inspire future generations to reflect on the poignant paradoxes that drive the artistic response to conflict.

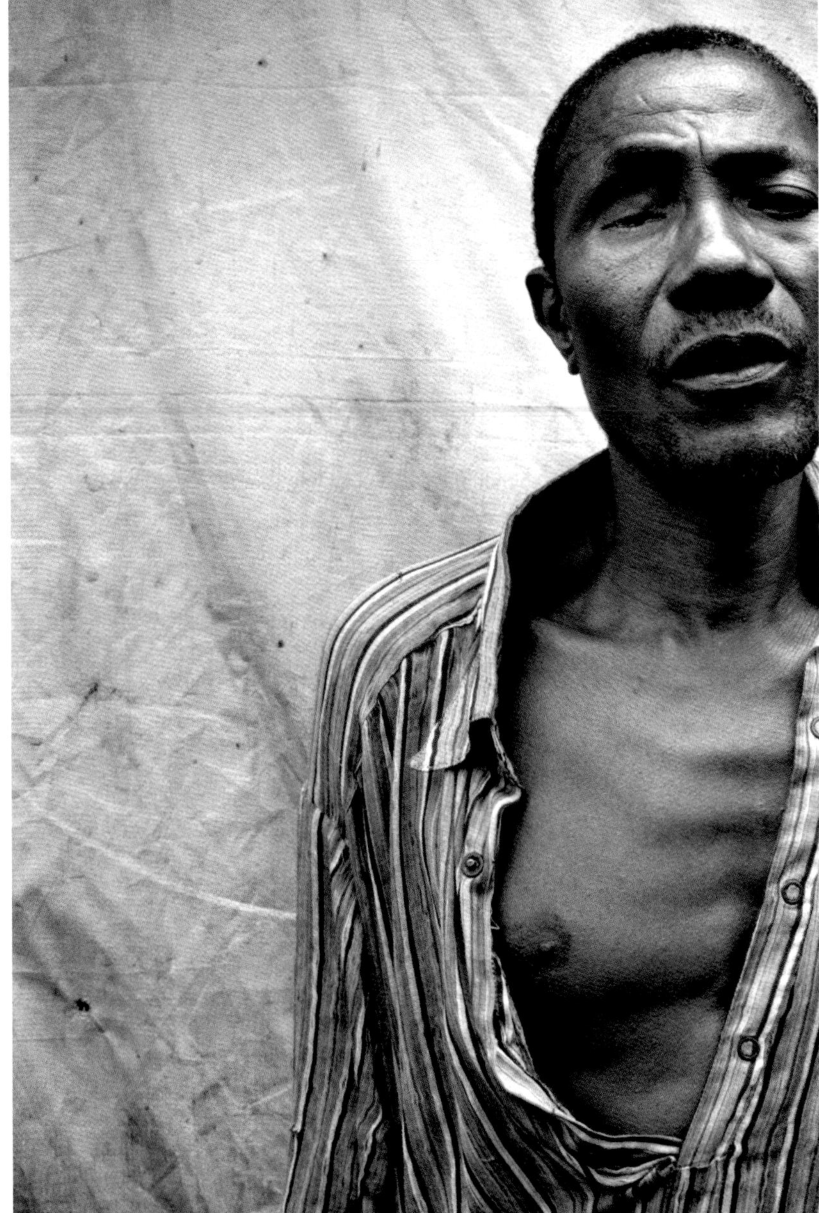

→

Tim Hetherington, *War Blind* series, 1999–2004

DIGITAL PHOTOGRAPHS FROM 35MM FILM BASE NEGATIVES

Photojournalist Tim Hetherington documented conflicts across the world. Aiming to depict 'real people in real situations', he explored life in times of crisis. Hetherington made a series of portraits of blind and partially sighted people in Sierra Leone, which engage directly with the idea of vision.

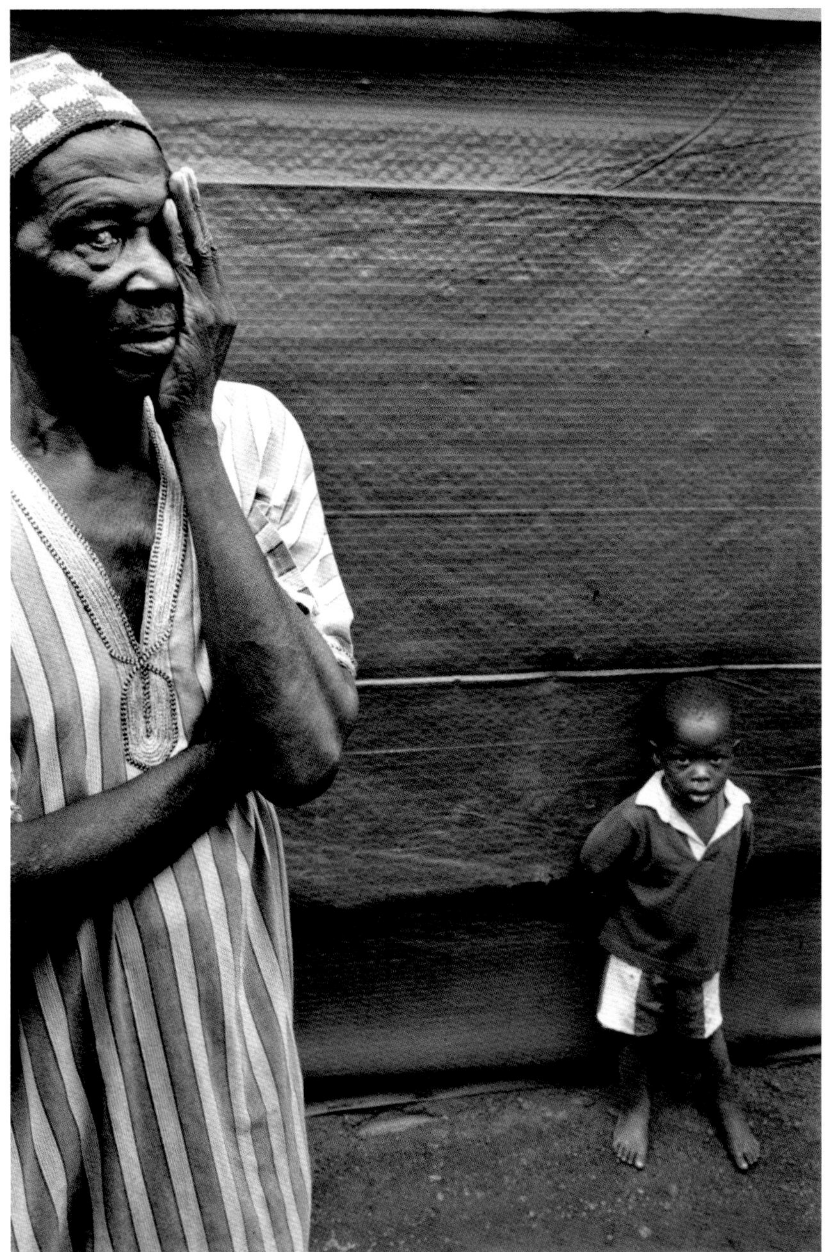

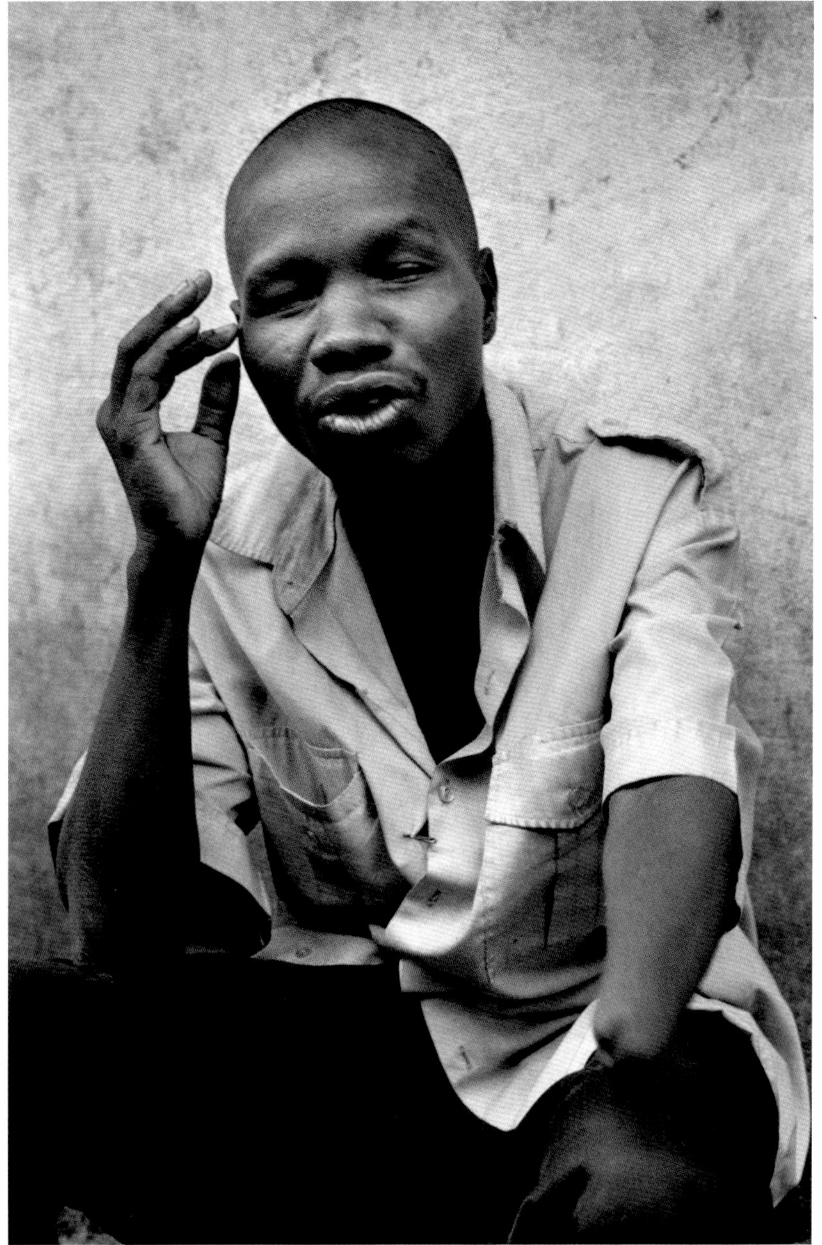

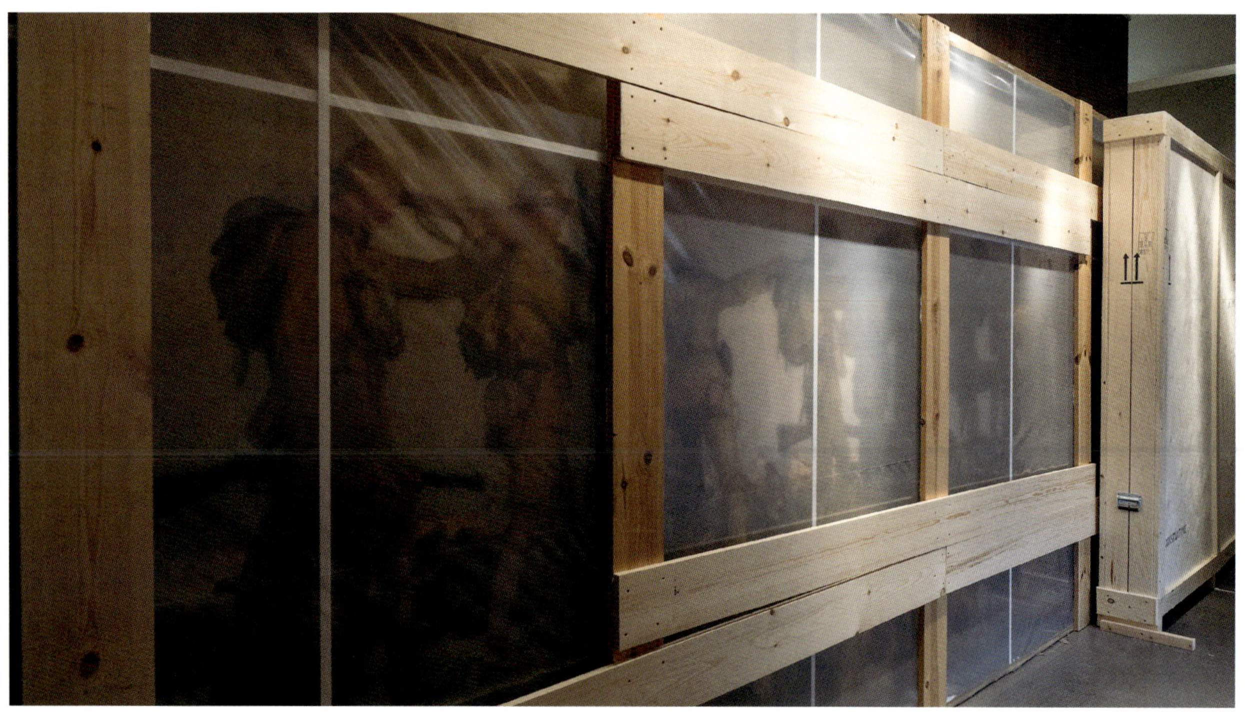

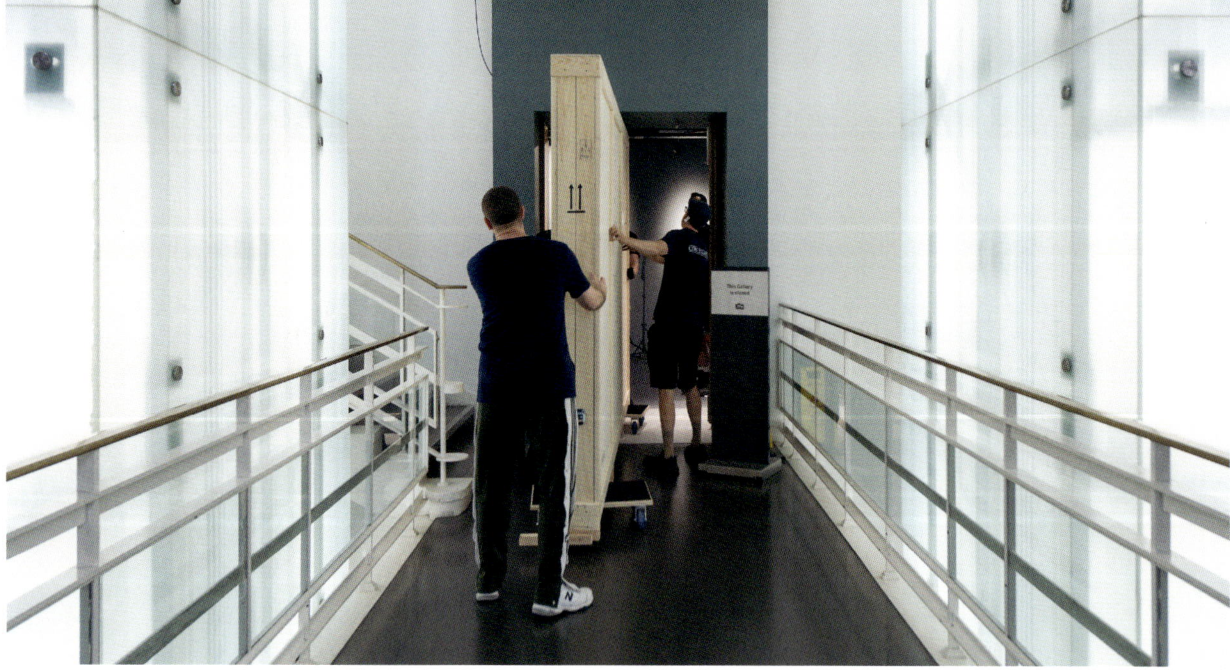

←→

IWM London, September 2023
Gassed is moved into position ready for re-display in the new Blavatnik Art, Film and Photography Galleries.

OVERLEAF

IWM London, September 2023
John Singer Sargent's *Gassed* installed in the Blavatnik Art, Film and Photography Galleries.

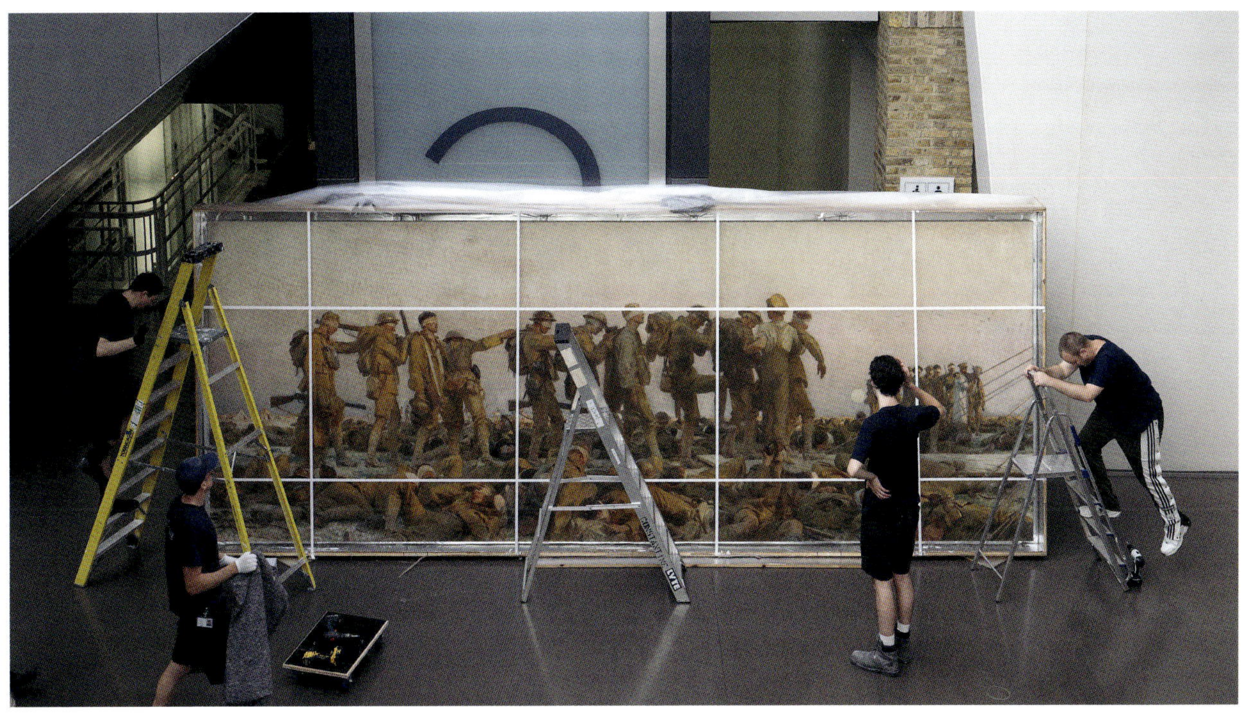

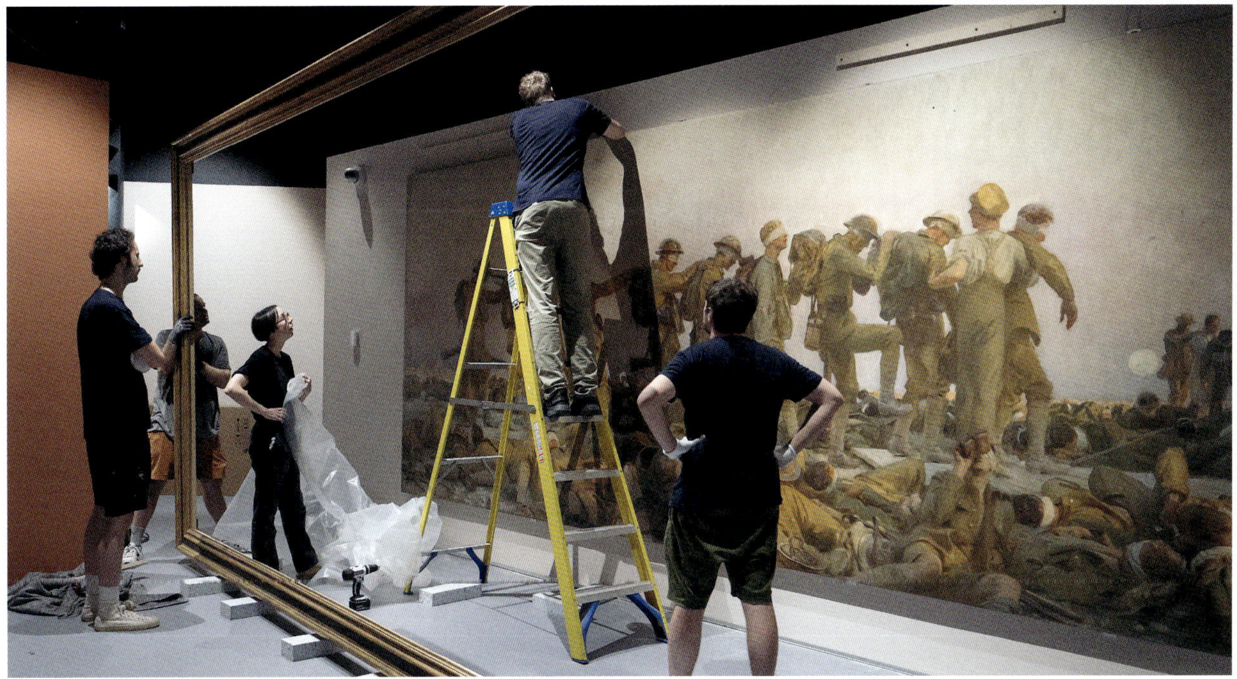

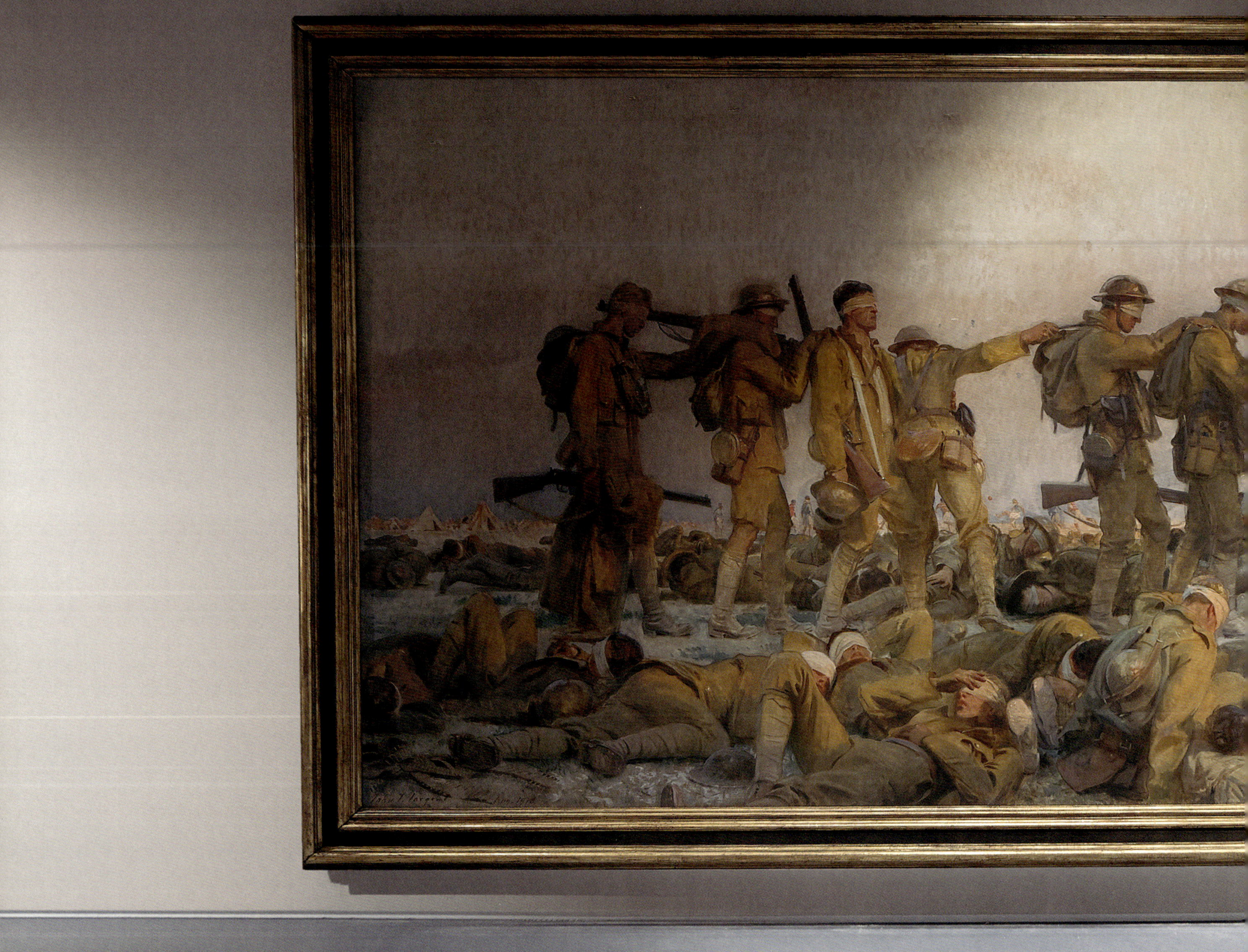

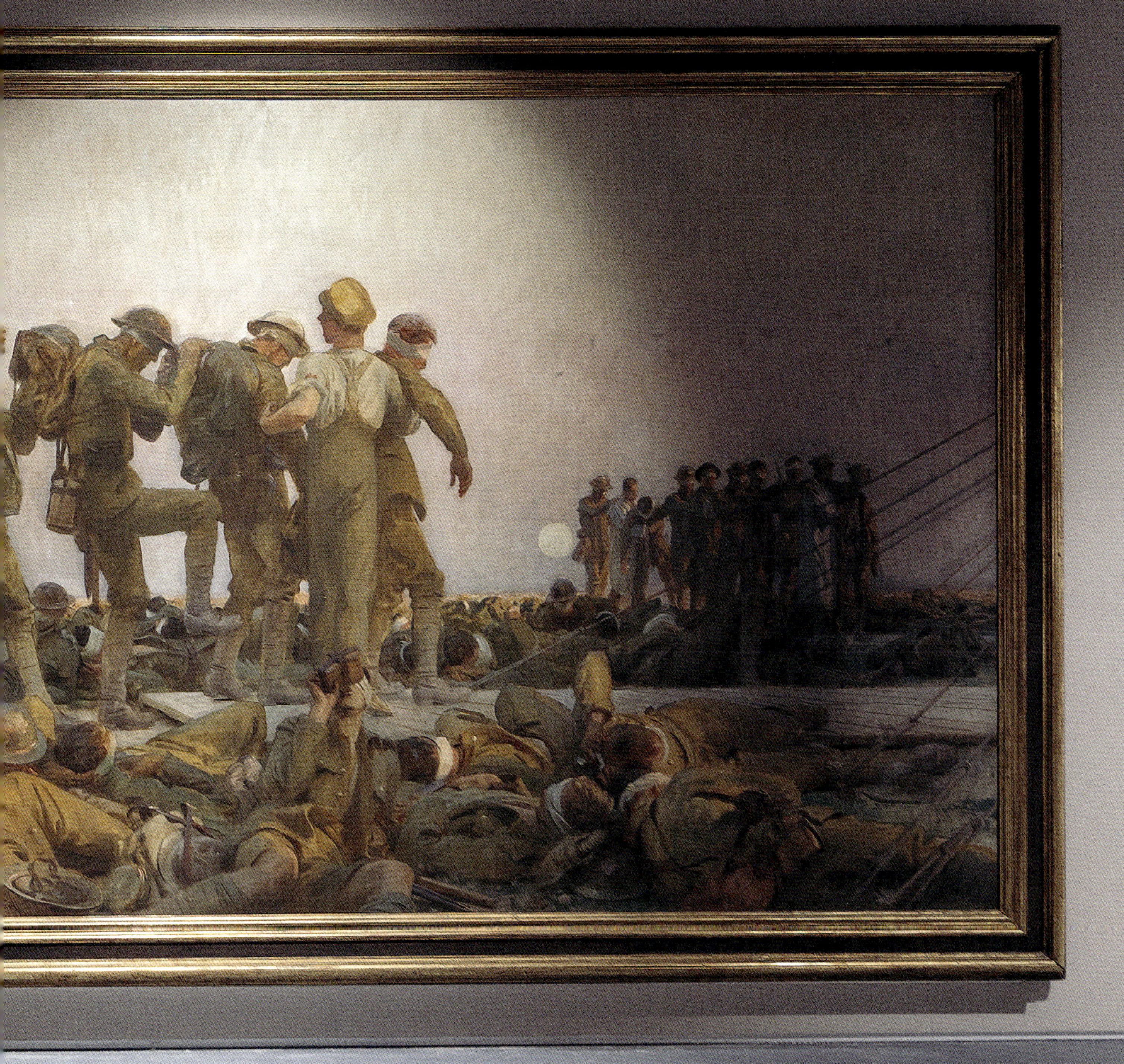

NOTES

'A Great and Lasting Service'

1 Official history statistics in terms of number of casualties are as follows: 1915: 5.79 per cent of wounds; 1916: 1.34 per cent; 1917: 9.29 per cent; 1918: 18.22 per cent. This gives totals of 185,706 casualties or 9.7 per cent of all battle injuries and 5,899 deaths (3.1 per cent mortality rate). Stats from *OH Medical Services, Statistics*, p. 111.
2 Claude Phillips, 'Royal Academy', *The Daily Telegraph*, 3 May 1919, p. 9.
3 Pamela Fletcher, '1919 – Virginia Woolf and Cocaine' in *The Royal Academy Summer Exhibition: A Chronicle 1769–2018*.
4 Virginia Woolf, 'The Royal Academy', *The Athenaeum*, 22 August 1919, pp. 774–76.
5 Pamela Fletcher, '1919 – Virginia Woolf and Cocaine' in *The Royal Academy Summer Exhibition: A Chronicle 1769–2018*.
6 'The Royal Academy', *The Morning Post*, 3 May 1919, p. 9.
7 Sue Malvern, *Modern Art, Britain and the Great War* (Yale University Press, New Haven and London, 2004), p. 93.
8 Elaine Kilmurray and Richard Ormond (eds), *Sargent* (Tate, London, 1998), pp. 23–24.
9 Claire Gibson, *Sargent* (Saturn Books, London, 1997), pp. 5–10.
10 Kenneth McConkey, *The New English: A History of the New English Art Club* (Royal Academy of Arts, London, 2006), pp. 29–30.
11 Trevor Fairbrother, *John Singer Sargent: The Sensualist* (Yale University Press, New Haven, 2000), p. 16.
12 Claire Gibson, *Sargent* (Saturn Books, London, 1997), p. 18.
13 Elaine Kilmurray and Richard Ormond (eds), *Sargent* (Tate, London, 1998), p. 16.
14 Sir Evan Charteris, *John Singer Sargent* (Charles Scribner's Sons, New York, 1927), p. 207.
15 Sue Malvern, *Modern Art, Britain and the Great War* (Yale University Press, New Haven and London, 2004), p. 75.
16 Sue Malvern, *Modern Art, Britain and the Great War* (Yale University Press, New Haven and London, 2004), p. 69.
17 Sue Malvern, *Modern Art, Britain and the Great War* (Yale University Press, New Haven and London, 2004), p. 76.
18 Sue Malvern, *Modern Art, Britain and the Great War* (Yale University Press, New Haven and London, 2004), p. 85.
19 Sir Evan Charteris, *John Singer Sargent* (Charles Scribner's Sons, New York, 1927), p. 214.
20 Letter from Henry Tonks to Alfred Yockney, Secretary of the BWMC, 19 March 1920, IWM Archive WA1/312/117.
21 Sir Evan Charteris, *John Singer Sargent* (Charles Scribner's Sons, New York, 1927), p. 215.

The Creation and Display of *Gassed*

22 Virginia Woolf, 'The Royal Academy', *The Athenaeum*, 22 August 1919, pp. 774–76.

Preserving for the Future

23 'Notes on John Singer Sargent's frames', from a revised version of a text written before the major Sargent exhibition shown at the Tate Gallery, Washington D.C. and Boston in 1998–9; September 1998, revised January 1999, May 2002 and January 2003.

PICTURE CREDITS

2, 6, 8 Art.IWM ART 1460 (details) © Factum Foundation for Imperial War Museums; 11 Art.IWM ART 1607; 12 Art.IWM ART 1611; 13 Art.IWM ART 1609; 15 Private Collection/Bridgeman Images; 16 Art.IWM ART 1460 (detail); 18 Museo di Capodimonte, Naples, Campania, Italy Mondadori Portfolio/Electa/Paolo Manusardi/ Bridgeman Images; 19 (left) Art.IWM ART 16162 9, (right) Art.IWM ART 16162 3; 21 Art.IWM ART 2242; 22 Art.IWM ART 192; 23 Art.IWM ART 2268; 24 Art. IWM ART 2243; 25 (left) IWM_2016_025_181, (right) IWM_2016_025_016; 26 © NPL – DeA Picture Library / S. Vannini/Bridgeman Images; 27 (above left) Art.IWM ART 1460 (detail), (above right) Art.IWM ART 1460 (detail), (below left) Art.IWM ART 16162 1, (below right) Art.IWM ART 16162 8; 29 (above left) WA1/312/164, (above right) WA1/312/166, (below left) WA1/312/166, (below right) HU 56114; 30 Art.IWM ART 1922; 32 Q 17028; 33 WA1/312/144; 34 (left) Art.IWM ART 17871 (detail), (right) DC 63657; 35 IWM_2018_073_0014_1; 36 (left to right) Art.IWM ART 1460 (details); 38 Art.IWM ART 1460 (detail); 41 (left) WA1/312/14, (right) WA1/312/4; 42 Art.IWM ART 1612; 44 (above left) Museo di Capodimonte, Naples, Campania, ItalyMondadori Portfolio/Electa/Paolo Manusardi/ Bridgeman Images, (above right) © NPL – DeA Picture Library / S. Vannini/Bridgeman Images, (below) Art.IWM ART 1460 (detail); 45 © Sheryl Lanzel; 47 Art.IWM ART 1610; 48 (left and right) WA1/312/117; 49 Q 11586; 50 (left) Art.IWM ART 16162 2, (right) Art.IWM ART 1460 (detail); 51 Art.IWM ART 16162 11; 52 (above) Art.IWM ART 16162 8, (below) Art.IWM ART 16162 1; 53 (above left) Art.IWM ART 16162 4, (above right) Art.IWM ART 16162 6; 54 (above) Art.IWM ART 16162 7, (below) Art.IWM ART 1460 (detail); 55 (above) Art.IWM ART 16162 10, (below) Art.IWM ART 1460 (detail); 56 Art. IWM ART 16162 12; 57 (above and below) Art.IWM ART 1460 (details); 59 Art.IWM ART 4032; 60 Art.IWM ART 4655; 61 Q 17028; 62–63 IWM SITE IWMN 2621; 64 IWM SITE LAM 226; 65 IWM SITE IWMN 2574; 66–69 Art.IWM ART 1460; 70 Art.IWM ART 1460 (detail); 72 Art.IWM ART 1460 (pre-conservation); 73 IWM 2023 003 0001; 74 IWM 2023 015 0027; 75 IWM 2023 015 0026; 76 (left) IWM 2023 003 0047, (right) IWM 2023 003 0128; 77 IWM 2023 003 0122; 78 IWM 2023 003 0109; 79 IWM 2023 003 0095; 80 IWM 2023 003 0090; 81–85 Art.IWM ART 1460 (details); 86–8 Courtesy Orbis Conservation; 89 (left) IWM 2023 036 0121, (right) IWM 2023 036 0128; 90–91 Art.IWM ART 17871; 92 DC 63657; 93 (left), DC 63660 (right) DC 63670; 94 (above) IWM 2023 052 0006, (below) IWM 2023 052 0015; 95 (above) IWM 2023 052 0052, (below) IWM 2023 052 0200; 96 IWM 2023 052 0215.

ABOUT THE AUTHOR

Rebecca Newell has been IWM's Head of Art since 2017, working on all aspects related to the care, display and interpretation of the museum's pre-eminent art collection. She was lead curator for the Blavatnik Art, Film and Photography Galleries, which opened in November 2023, and is also responsible for IWM's art commissioning programme.

ACKNOWLEDGEMENTS

For their support and contributions to this book, I would like to thank Phil Young, Hans Thompson and the wider Orbis team and the Factum Foundation team. I am very grateful to Richard Ormond for his illuminating and authoritative Foreword. I would also like to thank several IWM colleagues, including Caro Howell, Richard Ash, Victoria Singleton, James Taylor and Margaret Weller. Madeleine James and Lara Bateman from IWM Publishing shaped this book in important ways as did my editor, Catherine Bradley. Ocky Murray has created a wonderful design that really does justice to Sargent's work. I am very grateful to them all for keeping me on track.

Publication of this book coincides with the development and opening of the Blavatnik Art, Film and Photography Galleries at IWM London, which would not have been possible without Jo Burden, Jack Davies, Toby Haggith, Matt Lee, Helen Mavin, Geoffrey Spender and Iris Veysey.